"Ever since death became part of the [...] promise—through various messengers and means—that death will not be the end of life but rather its true beginning. From Genesis to the Prophets to the New Testament and everything in between, Jeff does a masterful job of showing us that for every believer in Christ, the long-term worst-case scenario is not gloom and doom but everlasting life to the full. In short, this is a book of hope."

Scott Sauls, senior pastor of Christ Presbyterian Church and author of *Beautiful People Don't Just Happen*

"Sometimes I discover a book that changes everything about how I thought about the subject of the book. Jeff Brannon's book, *The Hope of Life After Death*, is that kind of book. It is encyclopedic (everything you would ever want to know about the resurrection), biblical (a journey from Genesis to Revelation), and scholarly without being stuffy. But even better, it is filled with hope based in the reality of Christ's resurrection—hope for the world, for the church, and personal hope for me and those I love. If you're looking for some good news in what sometimes feels like a hopeless time, read this book. It (as does the resurrection itself) changes everything."

Steve Brown, author, seminary professor, and broadcaster with Key Life Network

"Dr. Jeff Brannon has given us a far-reaching explanation of the biblical foundations for the Christian confession, 'I believe in the resurrection of the dead.' He traces the developments of the themes of life, death, and resurrection throughout the Old Testament. He also examines how the New Testament proclaims that these themes are fulfilled in Christ and the general resurrection at Christ's return. His style will benefit both biblical scholars and motivated laypeople. It is a magnificent gift to us all."

Richard L Pratt Jr., president of Third Millennium Ministries

"Jeff Brannon's treatment of resurrection life more than amply provides what it promises: a biblical theology of resurrection, tracing the hope of resurrection throughout Scripture and redemptive history. Not merely a treatment of isolated instances of resurrections in the Bible, this rich study convincingly places resurrection squarely in the larger themes of creation and redemption. It inspires authentic hope of new life in Christ both in this life and in that which is to come. A refreshing and convincing read."

O. Palmer Robertson, executive director of Consummation Ministries

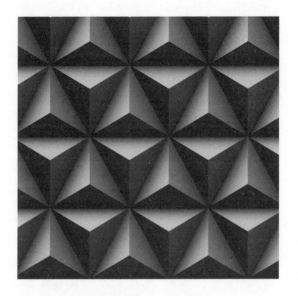

THE HOPE OF LIFE
AFTER DEATH
A Biblical Theology
of Resurrection

M. JEFF BRANNON

Academic
An imprint of InterVarsity Press
Downers Grove, Illinois

InterVarsity Press
P.O. Box 1400 | Downers Grove, IL 60515-1426
ivpress.com | email@ivpress.com

InterVarsity Press® is the publishing division of InterVarsity Christian Fellowship/USA®. For more information, visit intervarsity.org.

All Scripture quotations, unless otherwise indicated, are taken from The Holy Bible, New International Version®, NIV®. Copyright © 1973, 1978, 1984, 2011 by Biblica, Inc.™ Used by permission of Zondervan. All rights reserved worldwide. www.zondervan.com. The "NIV" and "New International Version" are trademarks registered in the United States Patent and Trademark Office by Biblica, Inc.™

"The Runner," copyright © Alex J. MacDonald 2008, used with permission. www.alexjmacdonald.co.uk/CD%20Lyrics.pdf.

The publisher cannot verify the accuracy or functionality of website URLs used in this book beyond the date of publication.

Cover design and image composite: David Fassett
Interior design: Daniel van Loon

ISBN 978-0-8308-5531-5 (print) | ISBN 978-0-8308-5532-2 (digital)

Printed in the United States of America ♾

Library of Congress Cataloging-in-Publication Data
A catalog record for this book is available from the Library of Congress.

29 28 27 26 25 24 23 22 | 8 7 6 5 4 3 2 1

For Colin, Drew, Evan, and Kate.

May you know and live in light of the hope of resurrection.

CONTENTS

SERIES PREFACE

BENJAMIN L. GLADD

THE ESSENTIAL STUDIES IN BIBLICAL THEOLOGY is patterned after the highly esteemed series New Studies in Biblical Theology, edited by D. A. Carson. Like the NSBT, this series is devoted to unpacking the various strands of biblical theology. The field of biblical theology has grown exponentially in recent years, showing no sign of abating. At the heart of biblical theology is the unfolding nature of God's plan of redemption as set forth in the Bible.

With an influx of so many books on biblical theology, why generate yet another series? A few reasons. The ESBT is dedicated to the fundamental or "essential" broad themes of the grand story line of the Bible. Stated succinctly, the goal of the ESBT series is to explore the *central* biblical-theological themes of the Bible. Several existing series on biblical theology are generally open-ended, whereas the ESBT will be limited to ten or so volumes. By restricting the entire series, the scope of the project is established from the beginning. The ESBT project functions as a whole in that each theme is intentional, and each volume does not stand solely on its own merits. The individual volumes interlock with one another and, taken together, form a complete and cohesive unit.

Another unique dimension of the series is a robust emphasis on biblical theology, spanning the entire sweep of the history of redemption. Each volume traces a particular theme throughout the Bible, from Genesis 1–3 to Revelation 21–22, and is organically connected to the person of Christ and the church in the New Testament. To avoid a flat biblical theology, these projects are mindful of how the New Testament develops their topics in fresh or unexpected ways. For example, the New Testament sheds new light on the nature of the kingdom and messiah. Though these twin themes are rooted and explored in the Old Testament, both flow through the person of Christ in unique ways. Biblical theology should include how Old Testament themes are held in continuity and discontinuity with the New Testament.

The audience of the series includes beginning students of theology, church leaders, and laypeople. The ESBT is intended to be an accessible introduction to core biblical-theological themes of the Bible. This series is not designed to overturn every biblical-theological rock and investigate the finer details of biblical passages. Each volume is intentionally brief, serving as a primer of sorts that introduces the reader to a particular theme. These works also attempt to apply their respective biblical-theological themes to Christian living, ministry, and worldview. Good biblical theology warms the heart and motivates us to grow in our knowledge and adoration of the triune God.

AUTHOR'S PREFACE

THIS BOOK REPRESENTS the fruit of my reflection on and investigation of the topic of resurrection. My interest in the topic began when a seminary professor stated that many Christians can articulate the importance of Jesus' sacrificial death on the cross but have an impoverished understanding of the importance of Jesus' resurrection from the dead. Although I would not begin a formal study of resurrection until many years later, I began to reflect on this topic and the importance of Jesus' resurrection from that point.

What began as a reflection on Jesus' resurrection led to the study of resurrection in the Old Testament and finally morphed into a biblical theology of resurrection. As I began to study the topic in earnest, I became convinced of a couple of things. First, resurrection is an essential and central doctrine in Scripture. Second, the hope of resurrection is inextricably linked with all other creation and redemption themes and doctrines. What I had previously perceived to be a peripheral doctrine that I was trying to make sense of came into focus as an essential doctrine that is indispensable for God's plan of redemption. My hope and prayer are that, in reading this book, you will also recognize the centrality and importance of resurrection for discipleship and for the hope we have as Christians.

In line with the other volumes in the ESBT series, my aim in this book is to trace the hope of resurrection throughout Scripture and redemptive history—from Genesis 1 to Revelation 22. My goal is that the book would represent serious reflection on how the doctrine of resurrection unfolds in Scripture that pastors and scholars could benefit from, but that it would also be accessible for all Christians to read. By and large, this book represents the fruit of my own study and reflection on Scripture's teaching on resurrection. In various places, I cite, quote, and interact with scholars who have emphasized similar points, but I am in very few places directly dependent on them. In keeping with the goal that the book be widely accessible, unless otherwise stated I have used the New International Version (2011) for Bible quotations and citations.

No book is ever completed in a vacuum, and I am exceedingly appreciative of those who helped bring this volume to fruition. My wife, Jennifer, and son Colin were my first readers and provided feedback and encouragement on the first drafts of my chapters. I am also thankful for friends and colleagues who provided feedback on all or parts of the manuscript. Joe Martin, Holly Carey, O. Palmer Robertson, Richard Pratt, Tom Wilson, and Stephanie Morton all provided invaluable insight for how the book could be improved and sharpened. I am particularly grateful for Ben Gladd, both for his friendship over the past ten years and for his editorial insight for the series and this book. Finally, Anna Gissing's editorial feedback helped bring this project to its completion.

God has richly blessed me with a wonderful family. I'm grateful for their sacrifices and support as they graciously allowed me the time to complete this book. Jennifer and my children—Colin, Drew, Evan, and Kate—are truly the greatest blessings God has bestowed on me apart from my relationship with him. I'm so grateful that Jennifer has chosen to join me in this adventure of faith, children, and life. Colin, Drew, Evan, and Kate are a constant source of fun, recreation, adventure, and humor. It is truly a blessing to be their father and to be a part of their lives.

Finally, I'm eternally grateful for my Lord and Savior Jesus Christ, whose resurrection seals my own. Only the one who was dead and is alive forever, the one who holds the keys of death and Hades (Rev 1:18), can bestow the hope of eternal resurrection life.

INTRODUCTION

There is a life no one can take.
There is a chain of love no one can break.

BUDDY AND JULIE MILLER

EMBLAZONED ON MANY T-SHIRTS, hats, coffee cups, and various other accessories is the expression "Life is good." This catchy slogan, which is also the name of the company that manufactures the products, captures the excitement, wonder, and enthusiasm of life. A wonderful time with friends and family. A hike in the mountains. A walk on the beach. The excitement of a new adventure. These experiences capture the spirit of this slogan, and we can agree that life is indeed good. Beyond this, almost all people recognize on some level that humanity's purpose is linked with "life." People in history have sought to obtain eternal life in various ways—from a religious belief in an experience of life after death to a quest for a fountain of youth. Even in modern culture, there are some who contend that a sort of immortality will one day be achievable through scientific advancement. All of this reinforces the notion that people on some level recognize that humanity was created for life.

But we also know that, in addition to the good times, life is filled with broken relationships, heartache, financial struggle, suffering, and most notably death. These difficulties remind us that not everything is right with our world, that life at times is "not good," and that quests for immortality in a fountain of youth or through scientific advancement are vain hopes. The reason for this tension we all experience is given in Scripture. God created a good world, but sin has disrupted the created order and led to the fall, which includes suffering and death.

Within biblical theology, it is common to understand the story of the Bible through three major movements in Scripture: creation (Gen 1–2), fall (Gen 3), and redemption (Gen 3:15 to Rev 22:21). In Genesis 1–2, after repeatedly saying that parts of his creation are "good," God affirms his entire creative work by saying that it was "very good" (Gen 1:31). But soon after creation, Adam and Eve's sin and failure lead to the fall. To be sure, there are still remnants of goodness in God's creation after the fall, but all of humanity is fallen in sin, and even all creation experiences the effects of the fall. In Genesis 3:15 God begins his program of redemption through the first preaching of the gospel and his promise that the offspring of the woman will crush the head of the serpent. What is so surprising is that God's plan of redemption is not accomplished all at once, but rather spans thousands of years (and counting). This unfolding plan of redemption is the story of the Bible from Genesis 3:15 to Revelation 22:21.

From the narrative of the Bible, the themes of life, death, and resurrection correspond with the biblical-theological categories of creation, fall, and redemption. God creates humanity and gives humanity life. With the fall, humanity experiences the consequences of sin in death. But the good news (exceptional news!) is that in his plan of redemption God promises to defeat death and bring salvation to his people. To be specific, God's plan of redemption includes resurrection for his people. By the term *resurrection* I mean God's act to raise his people from the dead to a bodily and glorified eternal life in the new creation.[1] The significance of this cannot be overstated. Salvation must involve being rescued from death, and salvation entails physical resurrection and new life in the new creation. God created us for life, death is the result of sin and the fall, and God's plan of redemption

---

[1]With this definition I do not claim that "resurrection" terminology in the Bible is limited to this meaning alone. The Bible often uses resurrection language to refer to other realities (e.g., the present spiritual resurrection of believers [Rom 6:13; Eph 2:1-5]). Rather, with this definition I emphasize the final fulfillment of God's resurrection purposes in his plan of redemption.

entails life after death, or resurrection. Indeed, the hope of eternal life is so essential to God's plan of redemption that Paul says it was promised even before creation (Titus 1:1-3). The good news is that God will "destroy" death (1 Cor 15:26)—through the resurrection of Jesus and finally through the resurrection of those united to him by faith. Whereas the thief comes to steal, kill, and destroy, Jesus comes to bring life (Jn 10:10). This life is nothing less than the abundant and eternal life that is inaugurated now but will reach its final fulfillment only in our resurrected and glorified bodies in the new creation.

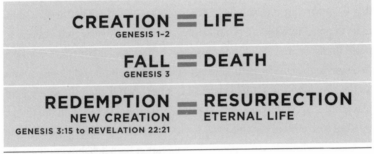

Figure 0.1. History of redemption

My interest in the topic of resurrection was sparked by two somewhat embarrassing but watershed realizations. First, I realized that I could not articulate a theology of Jesus' resurrection. In an introductory theology class in my first semester of seminary, the professor posed a question to this effect: "When asked about the meaning and importance of Christ's sacrificial death, most Christians can articulate a thoughtful and biblical response. When pressed to answer the question, 'Why is the resurrection of Christ important?' many Christians who could speak at length about a theology of the atonement are at a loss for words." I sat there for the next few minutes thinking that the professor had described me. I could discuss the importance of Christ's death but could say very little about the importance of Christ's resurrection.[2]

---

[2]Richard B. Gaffin Jr. notes that systematic theology has concentrated almost completely on Christ's sacrificial death as an atonement for sin and that the resurrection has been relegated primarily to an apologetic focus; see *Resurrection and Redemption: A Study in Paul's Soteriology* (Phillipsburg,

Second, I had an impoverished understanding of salvation and eternal life. Of course, I understood that I was a sinner before a holy God, that I needed to be forgiven of my sin and declared righteous before God through faith in Christ, that Christ's work was the only basis for salvation, and that faith in Christ led to eternal life. But my understanding of eternal life was deficient. In his book *Surprised by Hope*, N. T. Wright contends, "Some declare that heaven as traditionally pictured looks insufferably boring—sitting on clouds playing harps all the time—and that they either don't believe it or don't want to go there."[3] I'm ashamed to admit it, but that view was quite close to mine.

Kenny Chesney's song "Everybody Wants to Go to Heaven" demonstrates this all-too-frequent misunderstanding of eternity. Although Chesney sings that "everybody wants to go to heaven," he makes it clear that nobody is particularly excited about it. In this view, heaven and eternity are having a mansion in the clouds, getting wings and flying around, and having a halo. As the song describes, this existence is surely better than the alternative place, but it's certainly not exciting and perhaps not better than the things we want to experience in this life. My view of eternity matched the thinking of the song—I surely wanted go to heaven rather than hell, but I didn't want to go to heaven right away because of all I wanted to experience on the earth.

Sad to say, the view that eternity is an immaterial existence in the clouds is all too common among Christians. Moreover, as Wright notes, even when Christians speak of resurrection, they often use the word as a synonym for "life after death" or merely "going to heaven."[4] For this reason, believers need to know what the Bible teaches about resurrection and eternal life. The biblical hope and the biblical view of eternity is a new creation, a new creation in which God brings heaven to earth, a new creation in which heaven and earth are one. In the biblical vision of eternity, God will raise up believers who are

---

NJ: P&R, 1987), 11. Steven Matthewson and Adrian Warnock emphasize that the same imbalance—more attention given to Christ's death on the cross than to his resurrection—is present in the church; see Steven D. Matthewson, *Risen: 50 Reasons Why the Resurrection Changed Everything* (Grand Rapids, MI: Baker Books, 2013), 12, and Adrian Warnock, *Raised with Christ: How the Resurrection Changes Everything* (Wheaton, IL: Crossway, 2010), 59-62.

[3]N. T. Wright, *Surprised by Hope: Rethinking Heaven, the Resurrection, and the Mission of the Church* (New York: HarperOne, 2008), 20.

[4]Wright, *Surprised by Hope*, xii.

united to Jesus Christ by faith, and they will share in his glorified, physical, and bodily resurrection. The bodily resurrection of believers is an essential piece of God's redemptive plan. Believers will for all eternity do what God created them to do: glorify God by serving as his vice-regents and reigning over the new creation. When I realized this biblical vision, I thought to myself, *Now this is an eternity that I can get excited about.*

These two concerns, a theology of the resurrection of Jesus and a theology of the final resurrection of believers, provided the impetus for my interest in the topic of resurrection.[5]

FOCUS AND PURPOSE OF THE BOOK

While my journey began as a reflection on the importance of Christ's resurrection and the future resurrection of believers, it led to a study of resurrection in the Old Testament and finally morphed into a biblical theology of resurrection. In this book, my purpose is to trace and investigate the theme of resurrection in all of Scripture, from Genesis 1 to Revelation 22. I will demonstrate how the hope of resurrection is grounded in God's creation purposes and unfolds throughout redemptive history, culminating in the final resurrection at the end of the age. I will also show that the biblical hope of resurrection is inextricably linked with all of God's creation purposes for humanity, specifically a relationship with God, life in God's presence, and humanity's reign over creation as his vice-regents.

Such a study is important for at least three reasons. First, the doctrine of the resurrection has received much less attention than the doctrine of the atonement, at least within the teaching of the church. As a result, many believers are unable to articulate a theology of the resurrection. Second, the majority of projects on the resurrection are apologetic in nature, arguing for the historical resurrection of Jesus.[6] Apologetic studies are of great importance, but a defense of Jesus' resurrection is not the focus of this book. Rather, I will

---

[5] As we will see, these two topics are not unrelated since there is an intimate connection in Scripture between the resurrection of Jesus and the resurrection of believers.

[6] For defenses of and arguments for the historicity of Jesus' resurrection, see, e.g., John Stott, *Basic Christianity* (Downers Grove, IL: InterVarsity Press, 2008), 62-79; N. T. Wright, *The Resurrection of the Son of God* (Minneapolis: Fortress, 2003); Wright, *Surprised by Hope*, 53-76; Michael R. Licona, *The Resurrection of Jesus: A New Historiographical Approach* (Downers Grove, IL: IVP

assume and presuppose the veracity of Scripture, the historicity of the biblical stories, and the historicity of the resurrection of Jesus. Third, studies on the resurrection often focus only on particular parts or sections of Scripture, especially the Pauline corpus.[7] Therefore, in light of the topical or apologetic treatments of resurrection, a study of how the doctrine of resurrection develops and unfolds in Scripture is perhaps overdue.

In keeping with the ESBT series, what distinguishes this study from others is my purpose to trace the theme of resurrection throughout Scripture, from beginning to end.[8] With this approach, in addition to investigating passages that either explicitly teach or more subtly hint at resurrection, I will highlight trajectories of life and death in Scripture, which serve to connect God's creation purposes with God's plan of redemption. Moreover, I will demonstrate how the hope of resurrection is not an isolated doctrine but is intimately connected with other biblical themes and doctrines (e.g., relationship with God, God's presence, and the kingdom of God).[9] As a caveat, my focus in this book is explicitly on the positive or redemptive aspect of resurrection, or the resurrection of believers. Scripture is clear that there is a resurrection of both believers and unbelievers (see, e.g., Dan 12:1-2; Jn 5:29-30; Acts 24:15), the resurrection of believers to eternal life and the resurrection of unbelievers to eternal damnation, but the resurrection of believers is my focus.

Academic, 2010); Gary R. Habermas and Michael R. Licona, *The Case for the Resurrection of Jesus* (Grand Rapids, MI: Kregel, 2004).

[7] For studies on resurrection in Paul, see, e.g., Gaffin, *Resurrection and Redemption*; Geerhardus Vos, *The Pauline Eschatology* (1930; repr., Phillipsburg, NJ: P&R, 1994), esp. 136-225. Brandon D. Crowe provides a thorough study of resurrection in the book of Acts in *The Hope of Israel: The Resurrection of Christ in the Acts of the Apostles* (Grand Rapids, MI: Baker Academic, 2020).

[8] Although I will trace the theme of resurrection throughout Scripture, this book does not represent a comprehensive study of resurrection. The scope of the project did not allow for a discussion of every verse and passage related to the doctrine of resurrection. For more comprehensive studies of resurrection, see Wright, *Resurrection*, and G. K. Beale, *A New Testament Biblical Theology: The Unfolding of the Old Testament in the New* (Grand Rapids, MI: Baker Academic, 2011), esp. chaps. 8–11.

[9] This book by and large represents the fruit of my own study of resurrection in Scripture. I am indebted to N. T. Wright (*Resurrection*, 85-128) for bringing to mind many of the Old Testament passages that I investigated. After completing an initial draft of this book, I read Beale's *New Testament Biblical Theology* and was delighted to find that Beale also notes the close relationships between resurrection and other biblical-theological themes, especially the kingdom of God. I heartily recommend Beale's book for a more technical study of resurrection and its relationship to other biblical-theological themes. Brandon Crowe also notes the connection between resurrection and the kingdom in Acts in his book *Hope of Israel*.

THE IMPORTANCE OF RESURRECTION

Although it has often been neglected, the resurrection is of central importance within the biblical worldview.[10] The phrase "Jesus is risen" is a central confession in the New Testament and in the life of the church from the time of Jesus' resurrection. We cannot dismiss the significance of the change from celebrating the Lord's Day on the last day of the week to the first day of the week, the day that Jesus was raised to life.[11] In 1 Corinthians 15:1-8 Paul says that the gospel he preached is of first importance and that the gospel is intimately connected with the historical death and resurrection of Jesus. A few verses later Paul contends, "And if Christ has not been raised, our preaching is useless and so is your faith. . . . And if Christ has not been raised, your faith is futile; you are still in your sins" (1 Cor 15:14, 17). Without the resurrection of Jesus, there is no forgiveness of sins. Without the resurrection of Jesus, there is no salvation. In Romans 4:25 Paul emphasizes that Jesus "was delivered over to death for our sins and was raised to life for our justification." Shockingly, there is no justification of sinners without Christ's resurrection. Scripture is emphatic that the resurrection is of central importance for salvation and the Christian faith.

The doctrine of resurrection is also unique. When distinguishing the Christian worldview from other religious and philosophical worldviews, apologists often point to some fundamental differences between Christianity and other religions. For one, people stress that salvation in Christianity is by grace and through faith and not by works (see Eph 2:8-10), while salvation in other religions is by human effort or good works (or at least a mixture of grace and good works). John Frame has pointed out as another distinguishing characteristic that we find a personal and absolute God only within the Judeo-Christian worldview.[12] Within the Christian worldview, God is supremely sovereign yet also personal in his essence, actions, and relationships.

---

[10]See Paul Beasley-Murray, *The Message of the Resurrection: Christ Is Risen!*, The Bible Speaks Today (Downers Grove, IL: InterVarsity Press, 2000). Beasley-Murray contends that "the message of the resurrection permeates every stratum of the New Testament" and is of central importance in New Testament theology (20).

[11]See Wright, *Resurrection*, 579-80.

[12]See John M. Frame, *Systematic Theology: An Introduction to Christian Belief* (Phillipsburg, NJ: P&R, 2013), 38-39.

Similarly, the doctrine of the resurrection distinguishes Christianity from other religions in at least two important ways. First, only in Christianity is the "founder" or the primary teacher no longer in the grave. The founders of all other religions are dead and buried. In almost all cases, there is not even a claim to their resurrection. Yet in the biblical worldview, Jesus Christ is no longer dead. He is raised to life, he has appeared to many people, and his followers are adamant about the fact that he has been raised from the dead. Second, as N. T. Wright demonstrates, the doctrine of the resurrection is unique to Jewish and Christian thought. While many religions might espouse an immaterial existence after death, only within the Judeo-Christian worldview do we find the doctrine of resurrection as the reversal of death, with the hope of an eternal physical life after death.[13] Consequently, not only is the resurrection indispensable to the Christian faith; it is also unique to the biblical worldview.

Finally, Jesus' resurrection is of utmost importance for discipleship. This was true for the earliest disciples of Jesus. After abandoning Jesus and even denying knowing him before his crucifixion, Peter and the apostles are transformed from timid and fearful to bold and courageous disciples of Jesus after his resurrection. Indeed, Peter and the other disciples are willing to speak boldly in the threat of persecution and even to die for Christ.[14] Their boldness is undoubtedly connected to the doctrine of the resurrection—both the resurrection of Jesus and the future resurrection of those united to Christ by faith. The author of Hebrews describes it this way: "There were others who were tortured, refusing to be released so that they might gain an even better resurrection" (Heb 11:35). Christians can suffer and even die for Jesus because of the hope of resurrection. Jesus' resurrection and the future resurrection of his followers changes everything.[15]

---

[13]See Wright, *Resurrection*, 32-84, and Wright, *Surprised by Hope*, 35-40. Wright notes that the only possible exception is Zoroastrianism, but see his discussion in *Resurrection*, 124-28.

[14]See, e.g., Peter and John's refusal to acquiesce to the demands of the Jewish leaders to no longer speak or teach in the name of Jesus (Acts 4:1-22) and Stephen's speech to the Sanhedrin in Acts 7, which led directly to his death. In Acts 12 the apostle James is put to death by King Herod. Furthermore, from church history we know that all or almost all the apostles were martyrs for Jesus.

[15]For discussions of how the hope of resurrection is of central importance and "changes everything," see Warnock, *Raised with Christ*; Matthewson, *Risen*; Timothy Keller, *Hope in Times of Fear: The*

Within the biblical worldview, death is both the enemy of God and the enemy of humanity (see, e.g., 1 Cor 15:26). The serpent who first tempted Adam and Eve is also the thief who comes to steal, kill, and destroy (Jn 10:10). The story of the death of Lazarus in John 11 illustrates God's perspective and feelings about death. When Jesus arrives on the scene, witnesses the sadness of Mary and Martha, and is confronted with the reality of his friend Lazarus's death, he is emotional. Most of us are familiar with Jesus' sadness, which is reflected in the shortest verse in the Bible: "Jesus wept" (Jn 11:35). In this moment, Jesus demonstrates his feelings about death, the sting of sin, and the grief that accompanies the terrible reality of death.

But the story of Lazarus highlights another emotion of Jesus' that often escapes us: anger. Bible scholars have noted that the phrase "deeply moved" in John 11:33 and 11:38 carries the connotation of anger. In his article "Jesus Gets Angry at Death," J. Scott Duvall writes, "As Jesus goes to the tomb of Lazarus, he isn't just overwhelmed with sadness and grief. He's also righteous with rage. He's fighting mad. He's angry at sin, suffering, disease, and most of all, death! He's furious at these evil powers for hurting the people he loves so deeply."[16]

Jesus gets angry at death! His explicit description of his purpose in John 10:10 is noteworthy: "I have come that they may have life, and have it to the full." Death is God's enemy; he is troubled by it, grieves over it, and is angry at it. Indeed, Jesus' life-giving purpose is so essential to his mission that he is willing to taste death in order to defeat these great enemies of sin and death.

N. T. Wright contends, "Death is the last weapon of the tyrant, and the point of the resurrection, despite much misunderstanding, is that death has been defeated."[17] I cannot help but think about the words of Obi-Wan Kenobi to Darth Vader in *Star Wars: A New Hope*: "You can't win, Darth. If you strike me down, I shall become more powerful than you can possibly imagine." There is of course great irony in using this example because the post-death

---

Resurrection and the Meaning of Easter (New York: Viking, 2021); Sam Allberry, *Lifted: Experiencing the Resurrection Life* (Phillipsburg, NJ: P&R, 2010); Wright, *Surprised by Hope*.

[16]J. Scott Duvall, "Jesus Gets Angry at Death: John 11:38," in *Devotions on the Greek New Testament: 52 Reflections to Inspire and Instruct*, ed. J. Scott Duvall and Verlyn D. Verbrugge (Grand Rapids, MI: Zondervan, 2012), 47.

[17]Wright, *Surprised by Hope*, 50.

experience of Obi-Wan Kenobi is a sort of immaterial existence, which is precisely not the biblical view of resurrection. Nevertheless, Obi-Wan's words emphasize that he has a post-death hope that is greater than the threat of death from the tyrant Darth Vader.

To return to a more biblical illustration, the book of Revelation gives hope to God's people in the midst of persecution and the threat of death because Jesus has been raised from the dead and holds the keys of death and Hades (Rev 1:17-18). Satan is the great enemy of God's people, and he uses deceit and persecution (even to death) in his "fury" and attacks on believers (see Rev 12:12). But how can believers conquer this great enemy?

> They triumphed over him
>> by the blood of the Lamb
>> and by the word of their testimony;
> they did not love their lives so much
>> as to shrink from death. (Rev 12:11)

Believers are equipped not to "shrink from death" because of the wonderful hope of resurrection.

In their song "Rachel," Buddy and Julie Miller sing, "There is a life no one can take. There is a chain of love no one can break."[18] These lyrics express the truth that God's relationship with his people is stronger even than death, and this hope of life after death is what we will investigate and trace in this book.

---

[18]"Rachel," track 10 on Buddy and Julie Miller, *Buddy & Julie Miller*, Craft Recordings, 2001.

Chapter One

CREATION AND LIFE

Everybody wants to rule the world.

TEARS FOR FEARS

"BEGIN AT THE BEGINNING . . . and go on till you come to the end."
I suppose this advice from the king to the rabbit in *Alice in Wonderland* serves
as good advice for biblical theology. It might seem a bit strange to begin a
study of resurrection in Genesis 1, but the creation account lays the theological
foundation for the biblical hope of resurrection.

Let's begin by reflecting for a moment on a question: Why did God create
humanity? Not why in the sense of God's motivation for creating humanity;
in this sense we could affirm that God does all things for his glory (see,
e.g., Is 43:6-7), but could say little else. But rather why in the sense of God's
purpose for humanity. What were God's intentions and purposes for humanity? This is one of life's most important questions. While many religions
and philosophical systems do not have answers for this most fundamental
question, the Bible gives clear answers. I will begin by considering a truth
that is central to Genesis 1–2 and essential for the purpose of this book: God
created humanity for life. Subsequently, I will identify three additional purposes from the creation account that God intended for humanity and explain
how they are intimately connected with God's life-giving purpose.

GOD CREATES HUMANITY FOR LIFE

The very first words of Scripture, "In the beginning God created the heavens and the earth" (Gen 1:1), attest to the marvelous fact that God is the author of creation and the author of life. When the Lord encounters a "formless" and "empty" creation (Gen 1:2), he responds by giving form and content in the six days of creation. On day six, God creates humanity as the crown of creation. In Genesis 2:7 we read, "Then the LORD God formed a man from the dust of the ground and breathed into his nostrils the breath of life, and the man became a living being." God, the eternal one and the source of all life, breathes life into the man, which God had formed from the dust of the earth. As the author of creation, God is "life giving," and he brings forth life from that which is lifeless. Moreover, God's act of "breathing" life into Adam emphasizes the role of God's Spirit in bringing about life. In light of the theme of this book, it is essential to recognize that God created humanity for life.

Three additional creation purposes are closely linked with God's life-giving purpose.

God creates humanity for relationship with him (basis for life). Although its familiarity obscures its significance, the fact that God creates people to have a relationship with him is astounding. The trinitarian nature of God reveals that relationship and love are at the very essence of God.[1] Since people are created in the image of God (Gen 1:26-27), they are also relational and are created to have a relationship with God.[2] The early church theologian Augustine captured this truth with his famous line, "You have made us for yourself, O Lord, and our hearts are restless until they rest in you."[3] Created in the image of God, people are able to have a relationship with God—to know him, to speak to him, to hear his word, to obey him, to walk with him.

---

[1] See the discussion in Timothy Keller, *The Reason for God: Belief in an Age of Skepticism*, rev. ed. (New York: Penguin, 2018), 223-26.

[2] Although not the focus of this book, the first chapters of Genesis also make it clear that, in addition to a relationship with God, God created humanity to have relationships with other people. While God declared that his work of creation was "good" on several occasions and "very good" at the end of his creative work, in Gen 2:18 God says, "It is not good for the man to be alone. I will make a helper suitable for him." Although the emphasis in this verse is on the marriage relationship, it nonetheless demonstrates that God designed humanity to have relationships with other people.

[3] Augustine, *Confessions*, book 1, article 1.

In the creation account, God establishes the parameters of humanity's relationship with him. Although the term *covenant* is not used, many scholars recognize that the basic elements of a covenant are evident in the creation account.[4] O. Palmer Robertson has noted that at creation God establishes the fundamental life ordinances of work, family, and Sabbath.[5] Genesis 1–2 makes it clear that the Lord enters into and governs his relationship with Adam and Eve and subsequently all of humanity.

In addition to the basic life ordinances, God establishes the parameters for a right relationship with him, emphasizing the life-and-death consequences associated with this relationship. In his blessing and warning to Adam and Eve, God says, "You are free to eat from any tree in the garden; but you must not eat from the tree of the knowledge of good and evil, for when you eat from it you will certainly die" (Gen 2:16-17). If Adam is disobedient to God's command not to eat of the tree of the knowledge of good and evil, death will be the consequence. Alternatively, life is implicitly promised for obedience to God's word and command. From Genesis 2:15-17 we can infer that life is promised to Adam and Eve for obedience and death for disobedience.[6] From this analysis, two key points should not be missed: God created humanity for relationship with him, and life is linked with and is the result of a right relationship with God.

God creates humanity for life in his presence (locus of life). For part of my graduate studies, I had the privilege of living in Edinburgh, Scotland, for three and a half years. In addition to its amazing architecture and rich history, Edinburgh has numerous parks and green spaces throughout the city. Located a few minutes' walk from where our family lived, and just outside the city center, is the Royal Botanic Garden. Consisting of over seventy acres of landscaping, trees, plants, flowers, ponds, streams, and walking paths, the Botanic Garden is full of beauty. Whether we walked through the garden, fed the ducks, enjoyed a picnic, rested on the grass, or admired the view of Edinburgh

---

[4]See, e.g., O. Palmer Robertson, *Covenants: God's Way with His People* (Suwanee, GA: Great Commission Publications, 1987), 13-21.

[5]Robertson, *Covenants*, 13-19.

[6]Many Reformed confessions refer to this arrangement as the covenant of works; see, e.g., Westminster Confession of Faith 7.2.

Castle from the high point of the garden, a visit to the Botanic Garden was one of our family's favorite outings. Anyone who has set foot in a garden such as this one knows that it is a place of beauty and life.

Genesis 1–2 reveals an important truth: life is connected with a place. Specifically, life is connected with the place of God's presence. In the creation account, God gives Adam and Eve a wonderful place to live: the Garden of Eden. While I was always amazed by the life and beauty of the Botanic Garden in Edinburgh, I suppose it was no match for God's gift of Eden to Adam and Eve. The Bible describes Eden as a place of life, beauty, and vitality, filled with trees (Gen 2:8-9), rivers (Gen 2:10-14), and food (2:9). Additionally, the first chapters of Genesis clarify that Eden represented God's temple-garden, or his dwelling place on the earth. In Genesis 3:8 we read of God "walking in the garden in the cool of the day." Regardless of the precise meaning and use of this phrase, the implication is that Eden represented a place where God dwelled with Adam and Eve.[7] Moreover, scholars have recognized a connection between God's instructions to Adam and Eve for working the garden in Genesis 2:15 ("The LORD God took the man and put him in the Garden of Eden to work it and take care of it") and God's instructions for the priests and Levites and their work in the tabernacle (Num 3:7-8).[8] The first chapters of Genesis emphasize that Adam and Eve not only had a relationship with God but also dwelled with him, enjoying close, intimate, and unbroken fellowship with God.

Most significant for this discussion is that in the middle of the Garden of Eden was the tree of life (Gen 2:9). In the tree of life, God provided the way and the means for Adam and Eve, and their descendants, to live forever with God. Of course, also in the middle of the Garden of Eden, presumably near the tree of life, was the tree of the knowledge of good and evil (Gen 2:9). In their test of obedience, Adam and Eve were free to eat from any tree in the garden except the tree of the knowledge of good and evil. From the

---

[7] I understand Adam and Eve in the creation account to be real, historical people. Adam appears in numerous genealogies in the Bible (see, e.g., Gen 5:1-5; 1 Chron 1:1; Lk 3:38) and also represents the "first man" in contrast to the "last man" or "last Adam" (i.e., Jesus) in Rom 5:12-21 and 1 Cor 15:21-23.

[8] See G. K. Beale and Mitchell Kim, *God Dwells Among Us: A Biblical Theology of the Temple*, Essential Studies in Biblical Theology (Downers Grove, IL: IVP Academic, 2021), 12-15.

creation account, it is clear that God created Adam and Eve, gave them a wonderful place to live, and provided the opportunity for them to receive eternal life. The creation account thus reveals another astounding purpose for humanity: God creates humanity to dwell with him in his presence.[9]

God creates humanity to glorify God by serving as his vice-regents (purpose in life). In 1 Corinthians 10:31 Paul writes, "So whether you eat or drink or whatever you do, do it all for the glory of God." With this exhortation, Paul provides a fitting summary of humanity's purpose—to glorify God in all things. As the Creator and Sustainer of all things, as the eternal and infinite one, as the only one who is holy, righteous, good, gracious, loving, and just, God is worthy of all praise and glory. Since God is all-glorious and worthy of all praise and honor, people are called to glorify, praise, and magnify God.

The Bible is replete with passages that serve as exhortations to glorify God. By considering just a few, we can see that the Lord's name should be glorified (Ps 115:1), that all the nations will worship and glorify the Lord (Ps 86:9), that people are created and called for God's glory (Is 43:5-7), that it is God's plan for the earth to be filled with his glory (Hab 2:14), that the good works of believers should lead others to glorify God (Mt 5:16), and that God is worthy of all glory (Rev 4:11). In answer to the question "What is the chief end of man?" the Westminster Shorter Catechism reads, "Man's chief end is to glorify God, and to enjoy him forever."[10] The small sample above demonstrates that the writers of the Westminster Standards were not without justification in identifying this as the purpose of humanity. Paul's exhortation in 1 Corinthians 10:31 is a good description of God's purpose for people—to glorify him in all that they do.

This purpose for humanity to glorify God is evident in the creation account. When God creates humanity he says, "Let us make mankind in our image, in our likeness" (Gen 1:26). Let's reflect for a moment on the importance of

---

[9]For excellent studies of temple and the notion of God dwelling with his people, see Beale and Kim, *God Dwells Among Us*, and G. K. Beale, *The Temple and the Church's Mission: A Biblical Theology of the Dwelling Place of God*, New Studies in Biblical Theology (Downers Grove, IL: IVP Academic, 2004).

[10]Westminster Shorter Catechism, question 1.

images. The very essence of an image is to bring glory or honor to that which it represents. Commenting on the role of images in the ancient Near East, G. K. Beale notes that "to be in the image of a god meant that the king reflected the god's glory."[11] Although we are far removed from the culture of the ancient Near East, our modern culture still embraces the importance of images in different ways.

One of my favorite hobbies and pastimes is following Alabama football. In Tuscaloosa, outside Bryant-Denny Stadium, there are statues of Alabama football coaches who have won national championships. The statues of Wallace Wade, Frank Thomas, Paul "Bear" Bryant, Gene Stallings, and Nick Saban are memorials of these coaches and serve to bring them honor for their achievements in college football. Even in twenty-first-century Western culture, images are important. If this is true in modern culture and for statues of college football coaches, how much more is this true of the ancient Near East and biblical culture? As God's image, people are created to glorify him— to reflect God's glory back to him in all that we do.

The creation account also reveals that God created humanity in his image to glorify him by serving as his vice-regents.[12] In Genesis 1:26 God says, "Let us make mankind in our *image*, in our likeness, so that they may *rule*" (emphasis added). God is the great king of creation, and he creates humanity in his image to rule over creation. From the context of Genesis 1:26-30, creation in the image of God is connected with God's purpose for humanity to reign and exercise dominion over creation. In Genesis 1:28 God's words to Adam and Eve serve as a blessing and command: "Be fruitful and increase in number; fill the earth and subdue it." This command, sometimes referred to as the original commission, provides the biblical and theological foundation for the kingdom of God.[13] To be specific, Genesis 1:28 communicates how

---

[11]G. K. Beale, *A New Testament Biblical Theology: The Unfolding of the Old Testament in the New* (Grand Rapids, MI: Baker Academic, 2011), 31.

[12]John Frame describes the significance of humanity in the image of God in a similar way when he writes, "What Genesis 1:26-28 says is that God has made man like himself to equip him for his task as lord, a lord subordinate to God's ultimate lordship. So the image of God consists of those qualities that equip man to be lord of the world, under God." *Systematic Theology: An Introduction to Christian Belief* (Phillipsburg, NJ: P&R, 2013), 785-86.

[13]For more thorough discussions of the kingdom of God, see M. Jeff Brannon, "The Kingdom of God," *Biblical Perspectives* 17, no. 30 (2015), http://reformedperspectives.org/articles/jef_%20

humanity will serve as God's vice-regents and reign over creation. As humanity is obedient to the original commission, God's image increases in number (be fruitful and increase in number) and extends to the ends of the earth (fill the earth and subdue it). As God's image increases and goes to the ends of the earth, so also God's reign extends to the ends of the earth.[14]

The band Tears for Fears penned the song "Everybody Wants to Rule the World." I am a big fan of this song for a couple of reasons. First, I simply like the music and the song. Second, the lyrics get at something quite profound. I really do believe that everybody wants to rule the world, and I think that all people want to rule the world because this is precisely what God created humanity to do! God created humanity in his image to bring glory to him and to represent his kingship. By fulfilling the original commission (Gen 1:28), humanity would bring glory to God by multiplying his image and therefore his reign throughout the earth. And this represents God's wonderful purpose for humanity.

Table 1.1. Creation purposes (life)

Basis for life	Right relationship with God
Locus of life	God's presence in Eden / tree of life
Purpose in life	Reign over creation as God's vice-regents

SUMMARY OF CREATION THEMES

As we have seen, God's life-giving purpose is intimately connected with other creation purposes and biblical themes: (1) God created humanity for a relationship with him, (2) God created humanity for life in his presence, and (3) God created humanity to glorify him by serving as his vice-regents. I have referred to these other purposes as the basis for life, the locus of life, and the purpose in life. To further illustrate the close relationship between these purposes, I will reference a phrase that Graeme Goldsworthy,[15] and

---

brannon/jef_brannon.KingdomofGod.html, and Vaughan Roberts, *God's Big Picture: Tracing the Storyline of the Bible* (Downers Grove, IL: InterVarsity Press, 2012).

[14]For this understanding of the kingdom of God, I am indebted to Richard Pratt's teaching from his hermeneutics course, Reformed Theological Seminary, Orlando, Spring 2002.

[15]Graeme Goldsworthy defines the kingdom of God as "God's people in God's place under God's rule." *Gospel and Kingdom*, in *The Goldsworthy Trilogy* (Bletchley, UK: Paternoster, 2020), 54.

subsequently Vaughan Roberts, have employed. Roberts defines the kingdom of God as "God's people in God's place under God's rule and blessing."[16] As he demonstrates in his book, these themes are closely related throughout Scripture and the history of redemption.

To connect Roberts's definition with the discussion in this chapter, "God's people" corresponds to a relationship with God (the basis for life), "God's place" corresponds to life in God's presence (the locus of life), and "God's rule" corresponds to serving as his vice-regents (purpose in life). This leaves only the final part of the phrase, "and (enjoying God's) blessing." But we can see from Scripture that the greatest blessing that God gives his people is life. Not merely life in isolation, but life in relationship with him, life in his presence, and life with the privilege of serving as his vice-regents. While other books have traced the themes of God's people,[17] God's place,[18] and God's reign,[19] in this book I will primarily trace the theme of life, and specifically resurrection life after the fall, as the great blessing of God.

Table 1.2. Creation purposes restated

God's people	Relationship with God (basis for life)
God's place	Life in God's presence (locus of life)
God's rule	Serving as God's vice-regents (purpose in life)
God's blessing	Life / resurrection life

From the onset of creation, God's purpose for humanity was life. But the life that God gave to Adam and Eve at creation did not represent the final fulfillment of God's purposes. In light of the prohibition not to eat from the tree of the knowledge of good and evil and the original commission, God called Adam and Eve to submit to his word and to obey his command in order to experience the fullness of life that God intended. Specifically, the

---

[16]Roberts, *God's Big Picture*, 22. Roberts adds "and blessing" to Goldsworthy's phrase and sometimes supplements the idea with "enjoying" God's blessing.

[17]See, e.g., Benjamin L. Gladd, *From Adam and Israel to the Church: A Biblical Theology of the People of God*, Essential Studies in Biblical Theology (Downers Grove, IL: IVP Academic, 2019), and Robertson, *Covenants*. Robertson emphasizes, "'I will be your God and you will be my people' is the heartbeat of every divine covenant in the Bible" (5).

[18]See Beale and Kim, *God Dwells Among Us*.

[19]See again Goldsworthy, *Gospel and Kingdom*, and Roberts, *God's Big Picture*.

fullness of life that God intended for humanity is closely tied to the creation themes in Genesis 1–2.

First, with God's command not to eat from the tree of the knowledge of good and evil, the implication is that Adam and Eve were to undergo a time of testing and probation. At some point, if they had been obedient, this time of testing would have ended, and the ability to sin by breaking God's command would have been removed. On the one hand, it is unclear whether Adam and Eve were to eat from the tree of life once or continually. On the other hand, Scripture does not explicitly reveal when and how Adam and Eve would have completed their time of testing. In light of God's expulsion of Adam and Eve from the garden and God's protection of the tree of life (Gen 3:24), it is possible that the time of testing and probation would have been over and the reward of eternal life would have been bestowed if Adam and Eve had eaten from the tree of life.[20] Regardless, what should be evident is God's intention for humanity: obedience and eternal life.

Second, in light of the Bible's depiction of the Garden of Eden as the place of God's presence and God's commission for Adam and Eve to increase in number and fill the earth, God's purpose was for his people to make the entire earth his temple-garden and the place of his presence.[21] As humanity was faithful to the original commission, multiplying God's image and subduing the earth, the garden (which no doubt would have become a populated temple-garden) would extend to the ends of the earth. In this way, the entire earth would become God's temple, the place where God dwells with humanity.

Third, as Adam and Eve and their descendants were faithful to God's original commission, they would also extend God's reign to the ends of the earth. Since God's image represents his domain and his kingdom, humanity would extend his kingdom to the ends of the earth. On faithful completion of the original commission, heaven, as the place of God's reign, would come to earth, and heaven and earth would be one.

---

[20]This inference is supported by God's expulsion of Adam from the garden after the fall, when God says, "He must not be allowed to reach out his hand and take also from the tree of life and eat, and live forever" (Gen 3:22).

[21]See Beale and Kim, *God Dwells Among Us*, 17-26.

Finally, although not explicit in the Genesis account, if Adam and Eve had been obedient, they would have likely received a heightened experience of life—what we could perhaps term a "glorified life." Upon obedience and at the end of their time of testing, in addition to the removal of the ability to sin, Adam and Eve would have perhaps been rewarded with new and glorified bodies. In 1 Corinthians 15:44-47 Paul contrasts the pre-fall body of Adam with the post-resurrection body of Jesus. Adam's pre-fall body was "natural" and Adam "became a living being," while Jesus' resurrection body is "spiritual" and Jesus has become "a life-giving spirit." That Jesus' resurrection body is greater than the pre-fall body of Adam is clear from 1 Corinthians 15:44-47, but the passage also perhaps implies that Adam would have needed a new body even if he had not fallen in sin.[22] Thus, Adam in his pre-fall state, with a "natural body" (1 Cor 15:44) and "of the dust of the earth" (1 Cor 15:47), was likely not fit to enjoy and experience the fullness of God's presence. If this is the case, then upon passing God's test, Adam would have been blessed with a glorified body, a body fit to experience God's presence, a body fit for a glorified creation, and a body that was no longer susceptible to sin and death.

God's purpose for humanity entails life, and this life is expressed through a right relationship with God, access to God's presence, and service as God's vice-regents. God's goal for humanity is nothing less than a perfect relationship with God, the entire earth as the dwelling place of God, the entire earth as God's kingdom, and an eternal life where his people are no longer subject to sin and death and are fit to dwell in his presence. These purposes are closely connected throughout all of Scripture—in creation, in the fall, and throughout God's long and unfolding plan of redemption. Understanding the close relationship between these purposes is essential for a biblical theology of resurrection.

CONCLUSION AND APPLICATION

When we reflect on God's purposes for humanity, we are reminded of God's goodness. God is the author of creation and the giver of life. He creates

---

[22]See Beale's discussion in *New Testament Biblical Theology*, 41-45, 262.

humanity for relationship with him. He provides a wonderful place for his people, and he intends to dwell with his people in the place of his presence. Finally, God gives humanity the wonderful privilege of serving as his vice-regents and reigning over creation. All of this emphasizes God's good purposes for his people. In the midst of the sin, suffering, turmoil, and death that comes after the fall, we should reflect on the life that God gave to his people in creation and the life that God promises in redemption. As wonderful as the life that God gave Adam and Eve in creation was, it will pale in comparison to the life that God bestows on his people in glorification.

Chapter Two

THE FALL: DEATH AND GOD'S PROMISE OF REDEMPTION

Look around
and you will see
this world is full of creeps like me.
You look surprised.
You shouldn't be.
This world is full of creeps like me.

LYLE LOVETT

IN CREATION, God bestows on Adam and Eve the blessing of life. As God's covenant people, Adam and Eve enjoy access to God's life-giving presence in the Garden of Eden and are commissioned by God to serve as his vice-regents to extend his reign to the ends of the earth. Along with these wonderful blessings and purposes, God establishes the parameters of his relationship with them. When God commissions Adam to work and take care of his temple-garden (Gen 2:15), he gives an invitation and prohibition: "You are free to eat from any tree in the garden; but you must not eat from the tree of the knowledge of good and evil, for when you eat from it you will certainly die" (Gen 2:16-17). The wonderful blessings and privileges God bestowed on Adam and Eve should have led them to trust God, submit to him, and live by faith and gratitude. They should have trusted that the parameters given to them by a good, loving, and gracious God were actually for their good! Tragically, this is not how the story goes.

Despite God's wonderful blessings and his stern warning of judgment, Adam and Eve quickly turn away from God and his word.[1] Rather than submitting to the Lord, they are deceived by the serpent and disobey God's command not to eat of the tree of the knowledge of good and evil (Gen 3:1-6). While eating a piece of fruit might seem innocent, this act of Adam and Eve represents full-scale rebellion against the Lord. By turning away from the Lord's word and submitting to the serpent's word, Adam and Eve give their allegiance to the serpent and commit idolatry instead of trusting God, his goodness, and his good purposes. This rebellion against the Lord has disastrous consequences for Adam and Eve and for all humanity descended from them. In this chapter, I will discuss the tragic consequences of disobedience in the fall but conclude with the promise of hope that God provides in Genesis 3.

THE PENALTY OF SIN: DEATH

As we have seen, from the beginning, God emphasizes that death is the punishment and consequence for sin and rebellion against him (Gen 2:17). In Romans 6:23 Paul alludes to this creation warning when he writes that "the wages of sin is death." The Genesis account and the rest of Scripture make clear that this penalty was not only for Adam and Eve but for all humanity. In Romans 5:12 Paul writes, "Just as sin entered the world through one man, and death through sin, and in this way death came to all people, because all sinned." The sin and death of Adam, as the representative for all humanity, led to sin and death for all people.

With two options before them—the tree of life and the tree of the knowledge of good and evil (in addition to an entire garden from which they could eat)—Adam and Eve chose the tree that guaranteed death. No wonder Jeremiah 2:13 describes sin as forsaking God, the fountain of living waters, for broken cisterns cannot hold water. To turn away from God is to turn away

---

[1]For minor portions of material in this chapter, I draw from M. Jeff Brannon, "The Kingdom of God," *Biblical Perspectives* 17, no. 30 (2015), http://reformedperspectives.org/articles/jef_%20brannon/jef_brannon.KingdomofGod.html.

from the source of life. The insidious nature of this sin and rebellion leads to the ultimate punishment: death. In our relationships with God and in our struggle against sin, we would do well to reflect on what sin really is. Sin is turning away from the fountain of life and turning to something that will bring ruin and destruction.

In Genesis 3, death as the consequence of sin manifests itself in two significant ways. First, since humanity's relationship with God is broken, spiritual death is an immediate consequence. This is the implication of Genesis 3:8-10 when Adam and Eve no longer enjoy unbroken fellowship with God but instead hide from the Lord. This severed relationship with God is evident throughout the Old Testament. The description of humanity at the time of Noah is that "every inclination of the thoughts of the human heart was only evil all the time" (Gen 6:5). In Psalm 14:1-3 David speaks of humanity apart from a relationship with God in this way:

> The fool says in his heart,
>   "There is no God."
> They are corrupt, their deeds are vile;
>   there is no one who does good.
>
> The LORD looks down from heaven
>   on all mankind
> to see if there are any who understand,
>   any who seek God.
> All have turned away, all have become corrupt;
>   there is no one who does good,
>   not even one.[2]

In a somewhat humorous example, Lyle Lovett provides some insight into this human condition in his song "Creeps Like Me." He sings that the world is full of creeps (including him) and that we should not be surprised at this reality. Although the world and secular philosophy will at times trumpet their view of the inherent goodness of humanity, the sad reality of humanity's sin, brokenness, and depravity always rears its ugly head. This only confirms the biblical truth that spiritual death is a consequence of sin.

---

[2]In the New Testament, see Eph 2:1-3 and Rom 3:10-18.

Second, although in his mercy God does not take the lives of Adam and Eve immediately, death is now inevitable and will be the fate of every human outside God's miraculous intervention.[3] In Genesis 3:19 God says to Adam,

> By the sweat of your brow
>   you will eat your food
> until you return to the ground,
>   since from it you were taken;
> for dust you are
>   and to dust you will return.

This heartbreaking reality is driven home when Adam and Eve are banished from the garden and no longer have access to the tree of life (Gen 3:22-24). The experience of death is not immediate, but it is inevitable. The famous line from John Donne captures this reality: "And therefore never send to know for whom the *bell* tolls; It tolls for *thee*."[4]

After the fall, death is inevitable. Furthermore, the body that is corrupted by sin is perishable, weak, mortal, and subject to decay (1 Cor 15:42-53). After the fall, humanity experiences the effects of sin and death even in life. And life itself is now a gradual descent to death.[5]

Death as the consequence of sin is a terrifying and awful reality. The author of Hebrews describes the post-fall plight of humanity as "those who all their lives were held in slavery by their fear of death" (Heb 2:15). The fear of death is real because of the horrifying reality of death. All people know this on some level and manifest the fear of death in different ways, at times doing whatever possible to avoid death. The biblical teaching on the fall makes it clear that sin is a capital offense against a holy God, and that death is a

---

[3]See, e.g., Enoch (Gen 5:24) and Elijah (2 Kings 2:1-11).

[4]John Donne, "Meditation (17)," in *Devotions upon Emergent Occasions*, ed. Anthony Raspa (New York: Oxford University Press, 1975), 87. Emphasis original.

[5]As redemptive history unfolds, Scripture reveals a third manifestation of death as the consequence of sin: eternal death, or eternal punishment. This horrifying reality is referred to as the "second death" (Rev 20:6, 14) and is described as "everlasting contempt" (Dan 12:2) and "eternal punishment" (Mt 25:46). Perhaps the clearest description of this reality is found in 2 Thess 1:6-9, where Paul says that the consequences of sin include an eternal punishment away from the presence of the Lord and his glory.

horrible and serious consequence of sin. In the previous chapter, I identified three purposes that are intimately connected with God's life-giving purpose. As we will see, these other purposes are also affected by the consequences of sin and the fall.

Humanity's relationship with God is broken and severed. As a result of the fall, Adam and Eve (and all humanity as their descendants) now have a broken relationship with God. After their disobedience, rather than celebrating and rejoicing in their relationship with the Lord, they hide from the Lord among the trees of the garden (Gen 3:8-10). Whereas they previously enjoyed intimate fellowship with God, they now run and hide from him.[6] Consistent with the Genesis narrative, Scripture emphasizes that there is no one who seeks God and no one who does good (Ps 14:1-3). People outside a right relationship with God are dead in their transgressions and sins and deserve God's wrath (Eph 2:1-3). As mentioned, this severed relationship with God is nothing less than a spiritual death. After the fall, humanity is estranged from God. This is devastating because life is the result of a right relationship with the Lord.

Humanity is cut off from God's life-giving presence. Whereas before the fall Adam and Eve enjoyed access to God, after the fall the Lord banishes them from the Garden of Eden and positions angels and a flaming sword to guard the garden and prevent access to the tree of life. In reference to this judgment, four things are noteworthy. First, since death is the consequence of sin, Adam and Eve no longer have access to the tree of life and are consequently unable to eat from it and live forever (Gen 3:22-24). Second, God's judgment is also an act of mercy. It was a merciful act of God not to allow humanity to live forever in their sinful and broken state. Third, since Eden represented God's temple-garden and the place of his presence, God's banishment of Adam and Eve from the garden means exile from the life-giving presence of God. Here and in other places in Scripture, exile from the place of God's presence represents death. Fourth, whereas God's presence formerly was life giving, after the fall God's presence can also be a source of God's

---

[6]After the fall, not only is humanity's relationship with God severed; relationships with other people are also broken (see, e.g., Gen 3:12 and 3:16, and the tragic account of Cain and Abel in Gen 4).

judgment. Because of sin and a broken relationship with the Lord, an encounter with the holy God can lead to death.[7] These four realities demonstrate the consequences of sin and the horrifying prospect of being exiled from the place of God's life-giving presence.

Humanity does not glorify God by serving as his vice-regents. A final consequence of the fall is that humanity does not glorify God by serving as his vice-regents. Whereas God created humanity in his image to bring glory and honor to him, after the fall the image of God is marred and people instead seek glory and honor for themselves.[8] Cain's lineage in Genesis 4:19-24 represents a culture and people that do not seek God or glorify him, but instead seek to glorify themselves. In Genesis 11:4 humanity's desire is typified by this statement: "Come, let us build ourselves a city, with a tower that reaches to the heavens, *so that we may make a name for ourselves*" (emphasis added). The verdict is in. After the fall, sinful people do not glorify God but rather seek to promote and glorify themselves.

Coupled with the failure to glorify God is humanity's failure to serve as his vice-regents and extend his reign. Humanity's new motivation is self-glorification (Gen 11:4) and new goal is the propagation of a reign that is opposed to God and his purposes (Gen 4:17-24). One of the reasons the fall is so heinous is that Adam and Eve listen to the word of the serpent and submit to the serpent's reign rather than listening to the word of the Lord and submitting to God's reign. This rebellion allies them with the serpent as their master. Not only does the serpent's word become primary in their thinking; Adam and Eve decide that they, rather than God, are the final arbiters of truth and morality. Adam's sin demonstrates a reversal of the original commission in that humanity submits to the serpent, part of the creation that God called humanity to rule over (Gen 1:26-30). In the fall, Adam and Eve reject the Lord as their king and reject God's word as their standard for how to live.

---

[7]Consider, e.g., God's words to Moses when he says, "No one may see me and live" (Ex 33:20) and "My face must not be seen" (Ex 33:23). Consider also Moses' fear at being in God's presence (Ex 3:6) and Isaiah's reaction and undoing when he encounters the Lord (Is 6:5). In these instances, God makes provision for Moses' and Isaiah's sinfulness and their entrance into his presence.

[8]Although the image of God in humanity is marred as a result of the fall, all humanity is nevertheless still in the image of God; see, e.g., Gen 9:6, where post-fall humanity is described as in the image of God. The image of God is renewed in salvation (2 Cor 3:18).

This rebellion against the Lord has disastrous consequences for the original commission. For the man, labor will be marked by hardship and difficulty (Gen 3:17-19), complicating the task of subduing the earth and having dominion over it. The woman will give birth to children, but giving birth will be marked by pain (Gen 3:16), making the task of multiplying humanity and filling the earth more arduous. Furthermore, humanity will forever be split into two camps, one that submits to God and one that submits to the serpent (Gen 3:15).[9] The implication of this is of central importance: after the fall, the numerical (be fruitful and increase in number) and geographical (fill the earth and subdue it) expansion of humanity does not necessarily extend God's reign throughout the earth. This reality is evident from the account in Genesis 4–11 when humanity propagates what could be termed a reign of death rather than the reign of God. Whereas life is associated with God's reign, death is associated with and is the outcome of rebellion against God. For God to restore his people to his life-giving reign, the sin and rebellion of humanity must be addressed.

Table 2.1. Results of the fall (death)

CREATION PURPOSE	RESULT OF SIN
Right relationship with God (basis for life)	Separated from God / spiritual death
Dwelling in God's presence (locus of life)	Banished from the garden and God's presence
Glorifying God and serving as his vice-regents (purpose in life)	Failure to glorify God and serve as his vice-regents

GOD'S PROMISE OF REDEMPTION

As a result of the fall, humanity needs redemption. The first promise of redemption comes in Genesis 3:15 when God says to the serpent,

> And I will put enmity
>   between you and the woman,
>   and between your offspring and hers;

---

[9]In the New Testament, see, e.g., Jn 8:44, where Jesus declares to unbelieving Jews that they are of their father the devil, and Eph 2:2, where Paul describes the pre-Christian past of believers as following the prince of the power of the air.

> he will crush your head,
>   and you will strike his heel.

Theologians have referred to this prophecy as the first preaching of the gospel. This prophecy is good news indeed. God promises that the serpent will be crushed by the offspring of the woman. The promise that "he will crush your head" anticipates a singular figure who will ultimately crush Satan, but it is important to recognize that this prophecy also represents a promise of victory for humanity over the serpent.[10] In light of this first preaching of the gospel, it is important to note that (1) God's purposes for humanity do not change after the fall, (2) there must be redemption in order for humanity to accomplish its God-given purposes, and (3) the offspring of the woman will crush the head of the serpent and bring victory for all God's people.

God's first promise of victory after the fall implies and guarantees that his creation purposes will be fulfilled in redemption. First, humanity's relationship with God will be restored. Whereas there was alienation and brokenness after the fall, God's promise of victory ensures reconciliation between God and his people.[11] Since a right relationship with God is the basis for life, the unfolding of Scripture reveals that God's relationship with his people extends even beyond death.[12] Second, redemption implies that God's people will again dwell with him and be restored to the place of his presence. Third, redemption implies that humanity will once again glorify God by serving as his vice-regents and reigning with God. Finally, the first preaching of the gospel implies and promises that death, as the consequence of sin, will be undone. The promise of victory for God's people, then, can be nothing less than a life that conquers death.

---

[10]Although there are many allusions to the fulfillment of Gen 3:15 in Christ (e.g., 1 Cor 15:20-28; Eph 1:20-23), perhaps the most direct allusion is Rom 16:20, where Paul writes, "The God of peace will soon crush Satan under your feet." Here Paul emphasizes that all believers will have victory over Satan and will play a role in the fulfillment of Gen 3:15.

[11]Although not the focus of the book, God's promise of redemption also implies that there will be reconciliation within human relationships as well.

[12]That God's relationship with his people is so strong that it would extend beyond death is a theme that N. T. Wright emphasizes in *The Resurrection of the Son of God* (Minneapolis: Fortress, 2003); see, e.g., 108-28. Wright contends that the belief that God's "love and creative power are so strong that even death cannot break them" is foundational for understanding the biblical doctrine of resurrection (124).

The first preaching of the gospel has most often been interpreted as God's promise to bring redemption to humanity, and this hope is of greatest importance in biblical theology. My purpose here is to focus in on the redemptive aspect of life after death: resurrection. Understood in this light, the first preaching of the gospel in Genesis 3:15 is the first promise of resurrection in Scripture. In a similar vein, G. K. Beale traces resurrection back to the first chapters of the Bible when he writes, "The first possible hint of resurrection life may be discernible in Gen. 1–3. . . . The promise in Gen. 3:15 of the seed of the woman who would decisively defeat the serpent likely entails also an implicit reversal of his work that introduced death."[13] The doctrine of resurrection, as it unfolds in the rest of Scripture, can ultimately be traced back to God's first promise of victory. The first preaching of the gospel sets the stage for God's unfolding plan of redemption and the hope of resurrection life.

With the first promise of redemption, the close relationship between God's purposes for humanity comes into focus again. A right relationship with God is the basis for life, God's presence is the source of life, and serving as God's vice-regents represents humanity's purpose in life. In both creation and redemption, these purposes are inseparably linked to God's life-giving purpose. God's promise in Genesis 3:15 assures that these creation purposes for humanity will be fulfilled in redemption.

Table 2.2. Promise of redemption (eternal life)

RESULT OF SIN	REDEMPTION / REVERSAL OF THE FALL
Broken relationship with God	Restored relationship with God
Separation from God's presence	Restoration to God's life-giving presence
Failure to extend God's reign	Promise of reigning with God
Death	Resurrection life

A GLIMMER OF HOPE

Soon after the first promise of redemption, there are glimmers of hope in Genesis 3:20-21. Adam names his wife Eve "because she would become

---

[13]G. K. Beale, *A New Testament Biblical Theology: The Unfolding of the Old Testament in the New* (Grand Rapids, MI: Baker Academic, 2011), 228.

the mother of all the living" (Gen 3:20). The hope for God's people is that the offspring of the woman will crush the head of the serpent. With Eve's name, Scripture reveals and confirms how that promise will be realized. Eve will become the mother of all the living, and victory will come through her offspring.

In addition to the naming of Eve, God provides garments of skin as clothing for Adam and Eve (Gen 3:21). God's provision hints at what will become three significant themes in Scripture. First, God must deal with and cover humanity's sin and shame. Sinful humanity is helpless to restore its severed relationship with God. Second, God provides a sacrifice and substitute so that his people can live. Although death is now inevitable, the Lord takes the life of an animal to provide restoration for Adam and Eve. The provision of animal skins introduces another theme of utmost importance for the doctrine of resurrection: life is connected with a sacrifice. Third, the clothing that God provides hints at the future resurrection of God's people, and implies that the consequences of sin and death will be undone.[14] Whereas Adam and Eve are unable to adequately clothe themselves and deal with their sin and shame (Gen 3:7-10), God's provision implies that the curses brought on by sin and the fall will be undone through God's redemptive work.[15] These glimmers of hope reinforce God's promise to redeem his people and reverse the tragic consequences of sin and death through resurrection life.

CONCLUSION AND APPLICATION

From our perspective after the fall, it often seems that death is a natural part of life. But from the biblical perspective, death is not natural, death is an intrusion to the created order, and death is the great enemy of God and humanity. It seems that this truth is ingrained on our hearts and minds in some way, as the natural human reaction is to be afraid of death, to worry

---

[14]Beale, *New Testament Biblical Theology*, 228-29.

[15]That the provision of animal skins hints at future resurrection is supported by 2 Cor 5:1-5, where Paul describes future resurrection as being "clothed" with our heavenly dwelling rather than being "found naked" (2 Cor 5:3). Paul emphasizes that in this life "we groan and are burdened, because we do not wish to be unclothed but to be clothed instead with our heavenly dwelling, so that what is mortal may be swallowed up by life" (2 Cor 5:4).

about death, and, in many cases, to do whatever possible to avoid death. This is likely because our hearts and consciences on some level realize that God created us for life.[16] Moreover, through the heartbreak of death that we all experience, whether it be our own death or the death of a loved one, it is evident that death is a tragedy.[17] And our experience is confirmed by Scripture's teaching that death is the result of sin and the enemy of God and humanity.

But there is hope in the midst of the chaos and despair. This first preaching of the gospel promises redemption. God will restore his relationship with his people. God's people will experience life in his presence. God's people will reign with him. And God's people will overcome and conquer the great enemy of death. Just as these themes were closely tied together in creation and the fall, they will also be inseparably linked in redemption.

The reality of the fall and God's promise of redemption should instruct us in a number of ways. First, we should remember the seriousness of sin. Sin disrupted our relationship with the Lord and set humanity and all of creation on a trajectory toward death. Jeremiah's words should strike a chord with us: to forsake the Lord is to forsake the spring of living water and to turn to broken cisterns that cannot hold water (Jer 2:13). To forsake the Lord is to exchange life for death.

Additionally, we should reflect on God's grace and mercy toward sinners, even in the midst of our sin and rebellion. Rather than leaving us in sin, condemnation, and death, God promises to save his people. Not only is God the author of creation and the giver of life; he is also the author of redemption, new creation, and resurrection life.

Finally, the account of the fall should encourage us to repent of our sin and to turn to God for life. While death is the result of a severed relationship with God, life is found in a restored relationship with the Lord. To return to the Lord is to return to the spring of living water (Jer 2:13). And this is what

---

[16]In Rom 2:14-15 Paul makes it clear that God has written some truth on the hearts of all people and that they have an awareness of this truth because their consciences bear witness. Similarly, Rom 1:32 emphasizes that all of fallen humanity on some level knows God's decrees and knows that those who are in rebellion against God deserve to die.

[17]For the Christian, the only reason that death is not a tragedy is that Christ has conquered death (1 Cor 15:12-58; 1 Thess 4:13-18). This, however, is the subject of the remainder of the book.

God invites us to do—to return to him and to drink the water of life. In Revelation 22:17 we read, "The Spirit and the bride say, 'Come!' And let the one who hears say, 'Come!' Let the one who is thirsty come; and let the one who wishes take the free gift of the water of life." Our call is to return to the Lord and the water of life and to invite others also to drink.

Chapter Three

THE UNFOLDING PROMISE OF LIFE IN THE PENTATEUCH AND HISTORICAL BOOKS

Like the city that nurtured my greed and my pride,
I stretched my arms into the sky.
I cry Babel! Babel! Look at me now.
Then the walls of my town, they come crumbling down.

MUMFORD AND SONS

MANY SCHOLARS CLAIM THAT THE OLD TESTAMENT has very little to say about resurrection.[1] But the fact that resurrection is not as clearly elucidated in the Old Testament in no way diminishes its significance as a biblical doctrine. Many of the most precious doctrines of the Christian faith are only hinted at in the Old Testament, but then come to light in the New Testament.

When commenting on the doctrine of the Trinity, B. B. Warfield writes,

The Old Testament may be likened to a chamber richly furnished but dimly lighted; the introduction of light brings into it nothing which was not in it before; but it brings out into clearer view much of what is in it but was only

---

[1] It is not uncommon for scholars to highlight some debatable passages and conclude that Dan 12:1-3 is the only Old Testament passage that clearly communicates resurrection hopes.

dimly or even not at all perceived before. The mystery of the Trinity is not revealed in the Old Testament; but the mystery of the Trinity underlies the Old Testament revelation, and here and there almost comes into view. Thus the Old Testament revelation is not corrected by the fuller revelation which follows it, but only perfected, extended and enlarged.[2]

Warfield's comments on the Trinity are also applicable to the doctrine of resurrection. The hope of resurrection undergirds Old Testament revelation and at times comes into view, but is only fully revealed in the New Testament. In the next three chapters, I will trace the themes of life and resurrection in the Old Testament to demonstrate how they build on the creation purposes established in Genesis 1–3 and anticipate the fuller revelation of New Testament resurrection hopes. In this chapter, we will look at how the Pentateuch and historical books of the Old Testament reveal and anticipate the biblical hope of resurrection.

THE REBELLION OF HUMANITY (GEN 4–11)

As we saw in the previous chapter, the first preaching of the gospel in Genesis 3:15 implies and promises that the curse of death will be overcome and that God's people will experience resurrection life. The first preaching of the gospel represents the biblical and theological foundation for the hope of resurrection in the Old Testament. While this application of Genesis 3:15 has largely been overlooked,[3] the unfolding of Scripture and redemptive history lends credence to this view. In light of this, Old Testament believers could have had, and perhaps did have, some sort of resurrection hope. Moses sings about this hope in Deuteronomy 32:39 and gives voice to the Lord:

> See now that I myself am he!
>   There is no god besides me.
> I put to death and I bring to life.

---

[2]B. B. Warfield, "The Biblical Doctrine of the Trinity," in *The Works of Benjamin B. Warfield*, vol. 2, *Biblical Doctrines* (Grand Rapids, MI: Baker Books, 2000), 141-42.

[3]As noted, G. K. Beale also appeals to Gen 3:15 as an implicit promise of the reversal of death; see *A New Testament Biblical Theology: The Unfolding of the Old Testament in the New* (Grand Rapids, MI: Baker Academic, 2011), 228.

Hannah prays about it in 1 Samuel 2:6:

> The LORD brings death and makes alive;
>   he brings down to the grave and raises up.

While it is not possible to know precisely what Moses and Hannah believed about resurrection, their words demonstrate that Old Testament saints had some understanding that God can bring life after death, a belief that could be traced back to God's first promise of redemption.

The unfolding of redemptive history is a long process though. While Genesis 3:15 gives good news and the promise of victory, the trajectory of Genesis 4–11 after the fall is not a good one. We could even refer to it as a trajectory of death. A poignant example is the account of Cain and Abel. The story of Cain and Abel is likely included in the Genesis narrative to highlight a theme established in Genesis 3:15—the hostility between the offspring of the woman and the offspring of the serpent. Cain, who is undoubtedly allied with the serpent, refuses to heed God's warning and murders his brother (Gen 4:1-10). Whereas humanity previously felt immediate effects of the fall in spiritual death (Gen 3:8-11), separation from God (Gen 3:22-24), alienation from one another (Gen 3:12), and in the onset of decay, now humanity tastes actual death—in the form of violence from one person to another. Moreover, we see in Genesis 3–4 a pattern that continues throughout redemptive history: the serpent and the offspring of the serpent are associated with death, while God and the offspring of the woman are associated with life.[4]

The downward trajectory of humanity continues when we find a people and society in rebellion against the Lord. Humanity attempts to fill and subdue the earth, but not to God's glory and not under God's reign. John Frame notes this trajectory: "The cultural mandate does not anticipate the fall. But what happens after the fall? People still try to subdue the earth. In Genesis 4, we find the development of civilization among the descendants of wicked Cain. But they are not filling and subduing the earth to God's glory. So the result is wars, pollution, sickness, and so on."[5]

---

[4] Jesus' statement in Jn 10:10 ("The thief comes only to steal and kill and destroy; I have come that they may have life, and have it to the full") is an example of this stark contrast.

[5] John M. Frame, *Systematic Theology: An Introduction to Christian Belief* (Phillipsburg, NJ: P&R, 2013), 1035.

Again, the song "Everybody Wants to Rule the World" by Tears for Fears is insightful. Humanity desires to rule the world because God created humanity to rule the world. But after the fall, humanity does not glorify God or bring his reign to bear on the earth. Cain builds a city (Gen 4:17), and his lineage and descendants build culture through dwelling in tents, raising livestock, inventing and playing instruments, and forging tools (Gen 4:17-22). While culture, community, and society building were undoubtedly part of God's intention for humanity, the lineage of Cain demonstrates that his descendants pursued these activities not for God's glory and as God's vice-regents. They pursued them in rebellion against God as servants of the serpent.[6] Cain's violence, death, and destruction are amplified when his descendant Lamech boasts,

Adah and Zillah, listen to me;
    wives of Lamech, hear my words.
I have killed a man for wounding me,
    a young man for injuring me.
If Cain is avenged seven times,
    then Lamech seventy-seven times. (Gen 4:23-24)

The sinfulness of humanity reaches a climax in Genesis 6:1-7 with God's evaluation that "every inclination of the thoughts of the human heart was only evil all the time" (Gen 6:5). The Lord resolves that he will not contend with humans forever and decides to wipe humanity from the earth (Gen 6:3-7). The Lord's judgment of humanity through the flood provides another poignant picture of the reality that the wages of sin is death (Rom 6:23). After the account of Noah, in Genesis 11 all of humanity has a common language, has continued to move east, and has gathered together at a plain in Shinar. The motive of self-glorification, only implicit in Genesis 4, is now explicit in Genesis 11. Humanity's desire is to "build ourselves a city, with a tower that reaches to the heavens, so that we may make a name for ourselves," lest humanity be scattered throughout the earth (Gen 11:4).

In their song "Babel," the band Mumford and Sons sings about this spirit of pride, greed, and self-glorification that is present in all humanity, and the

---

[6]While the phrase "servants of the serpent" might seem harsh, this is the dichotomy that God establishes in Gen 3:15 and Jesus affirms in Jn 8:42-47.

only remedy for this sinful human condition is for the walls of this tower (literal in the biblical account and figurative in the song and in the sinful human condition) to come crumbling down. As a result, the Lord descends, confuses their language, and scatters them over the earth (Gen 11:7-9). The verdict is in: after the fall, humanity does not glorify God as his vice-regents, experiences broken relationships with God and others, and promotes a culture of violence, death, and destruction.

In the midst of this violence and death, there are glimmers of hope. After the death of Abel, Adam and Eve have another son, Seth, and with his birth "people began to call on the name of the LORD" (Gen 4:26). The birth of Seth signifies the beginning of a remnant of people who are identified with the Lord and the offspring of the woman. In the genealogy from Adam to Noah (through the line of Seth) in Genesis 5, we encounter a familiar and oft-repeated phrase: "Then he died." But in the middle of the genealogy, the description of Enoch is that he "walked faithfully with God" and "then . . . was no more, because God took him away" (Gen 5:24).

This brief account of Enoch is highly significant. Enoch does not experience death, because God takes him away. For those who lived at the time of Enoch, at the time of Moses' writing, or in the subsequent generations after Moses, consider the wonder, awe, and hope this act would inspire. Enoch's final home is not the grave but in God's presence. God's removal of Enoch from the earth hints that death will not have the final say for God's people and provides a mysterious preview of the hope of resurrection. Moreover, we see once again that the basis for life is a right relationship with God. With such a brief account, the words "Enoch walked faithfully with God" are undoubtedly important. Enoch was in a right and restored relationship with God, and this reality carries with it the hope of life after death. The account of Enoch provides the first glimpse in Scripture that God's relationship with his people is stronger even than death.

The account of Noah also includes hope in the midst of judgment. After the Lord decides to rid the earth of humanity, we read, "But Noah found favor in the eyes of the LORD" (Gen 6:8). God will wipe corrupt humanity from the earth, but he will save Noah and his family, along with some of every creature. This account of Noah is important for a number of reasons. First,

God provides salvation in the midst of judgment. God saves the lives of Noah and his family, and his salvation extends to the entire creation. As God promised in Genesis 3:15, death will not have the final word. Moreover, because Noah finds favor in the eyes of God, his life is spared, highlighting again the connection between life and a right relationship with God.

In the Noahic covenant, God commands, "As for you, be fruitful and increase in number; multiply on the earth and increase upon it" (Gen 9:7). The repetition of the original commission reaffirms God's purpose for humanity to serve as his vice-regents, even in a post-fall world. Also bound up in the Noahic covenant is God's institution of the death penalty as a protection for human life (Gen 9:6). This is perhaps a bit strange, especially to our modern sensibilities, but God institutes the death penalty as a life-giving and life-saving measure. Finally, God promises that he will never destroy all living creatures or the earth again (Gen 8:20-22; 9:12-17). Indeed,

> as long as the earth endures,
> seedtime and harvest,
> cold and heat,
> summer and winter,
> day and night
> will never cease. (Gen 8:22)

In this way, God's covenant with Noah serves as a covenant of preservation. God is committed to fulfilling his promise to bring victory for the offspring of the woman, and death will not have the final word for God's people and creation.

ABRAHAM AND HIS FAMILY (GEN 12-50)

Although its significance is sometimes missed, the story of Abraham is of monumental importance. I remember singing the song "Father Abraham Had Many Sons" and dancing around when I was a small child. Yet when I reflect back on that experience, I had no idea of the theological importance of that song—that God's blessing of Abraham would extend to all the peoples of the earth (Gen 12:3), and that this eternal blessing is received through faith in Jesus (Gal 3:26-29).

In Genesis 12 God chooses and identifies the family that will bring his redemption and blessing to the world.[7] In Genesis 12:1-3 we read,

The Lord had said to Abram, "Go from your country, your people and your father's household to the land I will show you.

I will make you into a great nation,
    and I will bless you;
I will make your name great,
    and you will be a blessing.
I will bless those who bless you,
    and whoever curses you I will curse;
and all peoples on earth
    will be blessed through you."

This passage highlights how God's redemptive plan will unfold. Through the repetition of words like *bless* and *blessing*, the Lord reveals his intention to bring blessing to Abraham, his descendants, and the entire world.

Significantly, there is a close relationship between God's promises to Abraham and the original commission (Gen 1:28). God's promises to Abraham include a great nation, land, and blessing for all peoples of the earth through Abraham. Just as the Garden of Eden was the starting place for Adam and Eve's commission, the land of promise is the starting place for God's blessing of the world through Abraham. God called Adam and Eve to "be fruitful and increase in number" (Gen 1:28), and God promises Abraham that he will become a great nation.[8] Just as God called Adam and Eve to "fill the earth and subdue it" (Gen 1:28), God also promises that his blessing of Abraham will extend to all peoples on the earth. God's promises to Abraham are also reminiscent of his promise of victory in Genesis 3:15 and include two groups of people: those whom the Lord will bless through Abraham and those whom the Lord will curse. Through Abraham and God's redemptive plan, God's people will be restored to him and to their calling to serve as his vice-regents.

---

[7] I draw minor portions of my discussion of God's blessing to Abraham from M. Jeff Brannon, "The Kingdom of God," *Biblical Perspectives* 17, no. 30 (2015), http://reformedperspectives.org/articles/jef_%20brannon/jef_brannon.KingdomofGod.html.

[8] God's promise that Abraham's descendants will be innumerable like the stars in the sky (Gen 15:5) brings home this point even more clearly.

Finally, in God's promises to Abraham, God's blessing is tied to a place. Adam and Eve experienced God's life-giving presence in the Garden of Eden but were cast out because of sin, but God will bring his people to a new place where they will once again experience his blessing and life-giving presence. God is committed to calling a new people to himself, bringing his people to a new Eden, and restoring his people in their role as his vice-regents. The promise of "blessing" for Abraham and his descendants is nothing less than a new life—a new life through a restored relationship with God, life in God's presence, and a life of serving as God's vice-regents.

Table 3.1. God's promises to Abraham

God's people	Abraham and his descendants; all nations blessed through Abraham
God's place	Land of promise
God's reign	Many descendants of Abraham; great nation
God's blessing	Life in the land

Almost all the heroes in the Bible have stories of wonderful faith yet also incredible failure. The story of Abraham is no different and highlights both his resolute faith in God's promises (Gen 15:6) and his wavering faith on many occasions (Gen 12:10-20; 15:8; 16:1-4; 20:11-18). The famous test of Abraham's faith occurs when, after many years of waiting and wondering how God would fulfill his promise, Abraham is called by God to sacrifice Isaac, the child of promise and only child of Abraham and Sarah (Gen 22:1-19). Of course, those familiar with the story know that God stops Abraham before he takes the life of his son Isaac. From a redemptive-historical perspective, this story represents an important picture of salvation. Bible scholars identify Abraham as a type (or picture) of God the Father, who is willing to sacrifice his Son, and identify Isaac as a type of Christ, who is willing to offer himself as a sacrifice. Thus, the Abraham-Isaac event serves as a picture of Christ's sacrificial death on the cross.

In addition to serving as a picture of Christ's death, the event anticipates the hope of resurrection. In Hebrews 11:17-19 we read, "By faith Abraham, when God tested him, offered Isaac as a sacrifice. He who had embraced the promises was about to sacrifice his one and only son, even though God had said to him, 'It is through Isaac that your offspring will be reckoned.' Abraham reasoned that God could even raise the dead, and so in a manner of speaking he did receive Isaac back from death." The author of Hebrews communicates that God's rescue of Isaac was a resurrection of sorts. Abraham was so confident in God's promises that he believed God could even raise Isaac from the dead.

In light of the ups and downs of Abraham's faith journey, his resolute faith in this event is somewhat unexpected. Perhaps Abraham reflected on his experience with God in Genesis 15 when God went through the pieces of the animals in order to confirm that he would fulfill his promises to Abraham. With the miraculous birth of Isaac, Abraham's faith is so resolute he is convinced that God will fulfill his promises, even if that means raising Isaac from the dead. In this way, Abraham's faith anticipates the hope of resurrection. In the Abraham-Isaac account, God provides a ram to sacrifice as a substitute for Isaac (Gen 22:13-14). Notably, this act of substitutionary atonement continues the trajectory established after the fall that life is connected with a sacrifice. In light of God's rescue of Isaac and the description of Abraham's faith in Hebrews 11:17-19, there is good reason to believe that the Abraham-Isaac event anticipates not only Jesus' sacrificial death but also his resurrection. Just as Isaac was saved *from* death, the "greater Isaac," to whom Isaac pointed, was saved *through* death by resurrection.

At the end of Genesis, the story of Joseph serves as an explanation for Israel's later situation in Egypt and encourages Israel to trust in the Lord, the one who can rescue them from their dire circumstances. Significantly, the story is another example of the Lord bringing life out of death. In Genesis 37, out of jealousy, Joseph's brothers (with the exception of Reuben) first decide to murder him, next to leave him for dead, and finally to sell him into slavery. Joseph ends up in Egypt, and even though he endures various hardships, the Lord prospers him, and he is eventually placed in charge of all of Egypt, second only to Pharaoh. Through the Lord's revelation and Joseph's wisdom, Egypt is able to prepare for a terrible season of seven years of famine.

For Abraham's family, now represented by Jacob and his twelve sons, the famine is so severe that Jacob must send his sons to Egypt to buy grain "so that [they] may live and not die" (Gen 42:2). With the famine, the family of Abraham, and God's covenant promises and plan of salvation, are in danger. Although Joseph has every right to be angry with his brothers, he forgives them and sees God's life-giving providence in the midst of their evil plans. In the climax of Genesis, Joseph reassures his brothers, "Don't be afraid. Am I in the place of God? You intended to harm me, but God intended it for good to accomplish what is now being done, the saving of many lives" (Gen 50:19-20). Joseph's story serves as a paradigm of God working good out of evil and bringing life out of death. This is of particular significance, especially in light of where the biblical narrative picks up next: Israel's enslavement in Egypt many years later.

EXODUS

At the beginning of Exodus, after hundreds of years in Egypt, God's people have grown from the family of the patriarchs (Abraham, Isaac, and Jacob and his sons) into a great nation. The language in Exodus 1:7 is reminiscent of the original commission (Gen 1:28) and God's promises to Abraham (Gen 12:1-3): "The Israelites were exceedingly fruitful; they multiplied greatly, increased in numbers and became so numerous that the land was filled with them." For the Egyptians, what began as a helpful and nonthreatening family has now turned into a threat to their nation and livelihood. In response, the Egyptians enslave the Israelites, oppress them, and work them ruthlessly. When the Lord continues to bless Israel, Pharaoh commands that all the newborn Israelite boys be put to death.

In this precarious situation, we are introduced to Moses, the person God will use to deliver his people from Egypt. Even the miraculous deliverance of Moses at his birth foreshadows God's intention to save his people from Egypt and the threat of death. In response to the Israelites crying out to God, God appears to Moses in the burning bush and commissions him to lead his people out of Egypt. In this theophany, God reassures Moses by telling him, "I am the God of your father, the God of Abraham, the God of Isaac and the God of Jacob" (Ex 3:6). God's word is meant to encourage Moses that he has been with Abraham, with Isaac, and with Jacob—and now he is with Moses and Israel. What is surprising, and would seemingly be lost on us if not for

Jesus' teaching, is that God's word to Moses also provides Old Testament evidence for the resurrection.

In a confrontation with the Sadducees, who did not believe in resurrection, Jesus appeals to Exodus 3:6 as convincing Old Testament evidence (and even more narrowly from the Pentateuch, the only part of the Old Testament accepted by the Sadducees) to prove the doctrine of resurrection. In response to their preposterous and entrapping question, Jesus says, "But about the resurrection of the dead—have you not read what God said to you, 'I am the God of Abraham, the God of Isaac, and the God of Jacob'? He is not the God of the dead but of the living" (Mt 22:31-32; cf. Mk 12:26-27; Lk 20:37-38). By proclaiming to Moses that he *is* the God of Abraham, Isaac, and Jacob (who have long since died), God conveys that these Old Testament patriarchs at present experience some sort of resurrection life.[9] God could have said that he *was* the God of the patriarchs, but he emphatically declares that he *is* the God of Abraham, Isaac, and Jacob. To dismiss this interpretation as exegetical wishful thinking is to dismiss Jesus' interpretation of the Old Testament. The significance of Jesus' interpretation is twofold. First, the earliest writings of Old Testament Scriptures teach and testify to the doctrine of the resurrection. Second, God's relationship with his people is stronger than death.[10]

Beyond Moses' call, we can observe five items of significance from the exodus event. First, the hostility between the offspring of the woman and the offspring of the serpent comes into focus again. Egypt's plan is nothing less than genocide. Through the murder of Israelite boys, they intend to wipe Israel off the face of the earth. Thus, Pharaoh and the Egyptians who participate in this attempted genocide are allied with the serpent. Following the tempting of Adam and Eve, and Cain's murder of Abel, this represents another attempt of the serpent to bring death to God's people. Without the family of Abraham, how will God accomplish his plan of redemption? God's deliverance of Israel from Egypt emphasizes God's commitment to protect and bring life to his people. God has promised that his blessing will be brought to the

---

[9]Whether the reference is to the intermediate state or the future glorified state, it attests to the reality and hope of resurrection.

[10]See again N. T. Wright, *The Resurrection of the Son of God* (Minneapolis: Fortress, 2003), 108-28.

nations of the earth through Abraham and his family. The exodus event reminds us that God is committed not only to Israel but also to his plan to bring salvation to all the peoples of the earth through Israel.

Second, the climactic event before Israel leaves Egypt is the final plague, in which God strikes down every firstborn son in Egypt (Ex 11:4-5). God provides for Israel by instructing them to place the blood from the Passover lamb on the door so that the Lord will "pass over" that door and not strike down the firstborn from that family (Ex 12:21-23). The Passover account is another example of a sacrifice and substitute that brings life to God's people.[11]

Third, God establishes his covenant with Israel and takes them as his covenant people (Ex 19–24). God previously entered into a covenant with Abraham and his descendants, and now the family of Abraham has become a great nation. In Exodus 19:4-6 the Lord says that Israel will be his "treasured possession," "a kingdom of priests," and "a holy nation." Out of all the nations, Israel receives the privilege of a restored relationship with God. God calls Israel to worship him and to remain faithful to him and his covenant.

Fourth, God's presence with his people is a major theme in Exodus. God promises that he will be with Moses and with Israel to deliver them. The pillar of cloud by day and the pillar of fire by night that lead Israel signify God's presence with them (Ex 13:21). At the end of Exodus, the Lord gives instructions for the construction of the tabernacle, which represents God's dwelling place on the earth and God's presence with his people. God will be with Israel as he leads them to the land of promise, and he will dwell with them there.

Fifth, Israel represents God's kingdom. In Exodus 19:6 God specifically refers to Israel as a "kingdom of priests." This is the first place in Scripture where God's people are explicitly referred to as his kingdom. God is at work to restore his purpose for humanity through Israel. Israel will serve as his vice-regents and be his kingdom people.

---

[11]I regret that because of space constraints I am unable to include Leviticus in this study. Nevertheless, the prescriptions for worship, ritual purity, and the sacrificial system in Leviticus emphasize two important themes: the importance of a right relationship with God for life, and the notion that life is connected with a sacrifice.

The book of Exodus shows that God is at work to restore his creation purposes with humanity in and through the nation of Israel. God establishes Israel as his covenant people. God purposes to dwell with his people in the tabernacle. God establishes Israel as his vice-regents and kingdom people. Perhaps this leads us to consider, *What about God's life-giving purpose?* What should have become clear is that the entire exodus story is a movement from death to life.[12] God delivers Israel from Pharaoh, and God's purpose is to bring Israel into the land of promise, a place of rest, a place of life, a place where Israel will dwell in God's presence and serve as his vice-regents. This theme comes into clearer focus in the book of Deuteronomy.

DEUTERONOMY

After the first generation fails to trust God and take the land of Canaan (as recounted in Numbers), Israel finds itself forty years later on the plains of Moab just outside the land of promise (Deut 1:1-3). As we have seen, the exodus event represents a movement from death to life, and the book of Deuteronomy emphasizes God's intention not only to remove Israel from Egypt as the place of death but also to bring Israel into a place of life.

The Bible often describes the land of Canaan as a place of rest and salvation. The book of Deuteronomy also connects this land of promise with life. Before embarking on their entrance into the land, Moses writes Deuteronomy to lead Israel in covenant renewal. He reiterates that obedience to the Lord will lead to long life in the land (Deut 4:39-40), while disobedience will lead to disinheritance of the land, death, and destruction (Deut 4:25-27). Deuteronomy is so replete with these themes that space prohibits an investigation of the many references.[13] But one passage in particular, Deuteronomy 30:11-20, accentuates these themes and is worthy of a closer look.

In Deuteronomy 30:11-20 there is a clear contrast between life and death. Through faithfulness to the Lord, Israel can choose and find life in the land,

---

[12]For a thorough examination of this motif, see L. Michael Morales, *Exodus Old and New: A Biblical Theology of Redemption*, Essential Studies in Biblical Theology (Downers Grove, IL: IVP Academic, 2020).

[13]See, e.g., Deut 4:25-40; 5:32-33; 6:1-3, 24; 11:8-32; 12:1-11; 16:20; 28:1-68; 30:11-20; 32:33-37.

but through disobedience they will disinherit the land and find death and destruction (Deut 30:15-18). With language reminiscent of Genesis 1–2 and the Garden of Eden, Moses wants Israel to see that God is leading his people back to a place of life and the place of his presence. The picture that Moses paints in the Pentateuch is that entrance into the land of promise is a return to Eden. His description of the land as the mountain of (God's) inheritance, the place of God's dwelling, and the sanctuary the Lord established (Ex 15:17) echoes the description of Eden in Genesis 2. Furthermore, his description of the land as good and as a place of abundance is reminiscent of his description of Eden in Genesis 1–2 (Deut 4:22; 8:6-10; 11:8-15).[14]

Table 3.2. Redemption for Israel in Exodus and Deuteronomy

DEATH	LIFE
Enslaved people	Restored relationship with God / God's covenant people
No access to God's presence	Life in God's presence (tabernacle / land of promise)
Servant to Pharaoh/Egypt	Israel as God's kingdom
Slavery/persecution/genocide	Redemption / exodus / life in the land

In this new place of God's presence, God's people will enjoy a restored relationship with him, serve as his vice-regents, and receive the wonderful blessing of life in the land. Whereas God previously established his relationship with Israel as his people, established his presence in the tabernacle, and identified Israel as his kingdom people, the book of Deuteronomy clarifies that the land of promise is a return to God's presence and a return to a place of life. This reinforces that the entire movement from Egypt into the land of promise is a movement from death to life. And it is of no minor significance that all God's creation and purposes are closely linked in this movement from death to life.

---

[14]See the discussion of Oren R. Martin in *Bound for the Promised Land: The Land Promise in God's Redemptive Plan*, New Studies in Biblical Theology (Downers Grove, IL: InterVarsity Press, 2015), 77-86.

THE OLD TESTAMENT HISTORICAL BOOKS

The book of Joshua continues the story begun in the Pentateuch. Moses was God's servant to lead Israel out of Egypt, but God calls Joshua to lead Israel into the land of promise. Names in the Bible often have great significance, and the name Joshua in Hebrew means "God saves." Joshua is the one who will lead Israel to God's salvation—namely, entrance into the land of promise, a place of rest and life for God's people. Whereas Moses delivers God's people from the threat of death in the exodus, Joshua leads God's people into a place of life. In the history of redemption, Joshua's salvation anticipates the salvation of a greater and future "Joshua," the Lord Jesus Christ.[15] Moreover, as we will see in chapter five, the land of promise serves as an Old Testament picture of the new creation, and the abundant life that Israel is to experience in the land of promise anticipates the resurrection life that God will give to his people in the new creation.

In the history of redemption, God's covenant with David in 2 Samuel 7:8-16 is of utmost importance. This covenant builds on the redemptive trajectory of the Old Testament in a number of ways. First, we see how God continues to restore his relationship with his people. God's purpose is to provide his people with "a home of their own" where "wicked people will not oppress them anymore" (2 Sam 7:10) and where God "will also give [them] rest from all [their] enemies" (2 Sam 7:11). Second, God's plan of redemption is intimately connected with the place of his presence. On the one hand, God will plant his people in "a home of their own"—namely, the land of promise. On the other hand, David's offspring will build a house for God's name (2 Sam 7:12-13). God intends to dwell with his people in and through the temple. Third, the Davidic dynasty gives more shape and clarity to humanity's purpose of serving as God's vice-regents. Israel represents the kingdom of God (Ex 19:6), but a king from the line of David will lead God's people and bring God's redemptive promises to fulfillment. Fourth, the Davidic

---

[15]In the history of redemption, Joshua serves as a type of Jesus, and the land of promise serves as a type of the new creation. But whereas Joshua provides temporal salvation, rest, and life, Jesus brings his people into the consummate land of promise, the place of eternal salvation, eternal rest, and eternal life. For a thorough study of the motif of the land of promise as a type of the new creation, see Martin, *Bound for the Promised Land*.

dynasty will be the conduit for God to bring life to his people. God's promise to plant and protect his people in the land (2 Sam 7:10) implies a life of abundance in the land. In 2 Samuel 7:8-16 this means protection and flourishing in the old covenant, but this experience of life in the old covenant will find a greater fulfillment in the reign of the final and ultimate son of David.

Solomon ascends to the throne after his father David, with a glorious beginning to his reign. In addition to Solomon's building of the temple, there are glimpses of God's kingdom going to the ends of the earth through the expansion of Israel's borders (1 Kings 4:21) and through the nations recognizing Solomon's kingship and the goodness of the Lord (1 Kings 4:31-34; 10:1-13). Psalm 72 encapsulates the hopes, aspirations, and expectations of Israel under the reign of Solomon. These hopes are summarized in verse 17:

> May his name endure forever;
>> may it continue as long as the sun.
>
> Then all nations will be blessed through him,
>> and they will call him blessed.

Continuing the trajectory established in creation and with Abraham, the kingdom of God under the Davidic dynasty is to extend to the ends of the earth and be a source of blessing for all nations of the world. As Scripture reveals, though, the story of Israel is not always a good and happy one.

Because of Solomon's sin, God brings judgment on Israel, and the nation is divided into the northern kingdom of Israel and the southern kingdom of Judah (1 Kings 11:1-13). Although Israel suffers God's judgment, there are instances of God's grace and miraculous power during this time of the divided kingdom. The ministries of Elijah and Elisha are particularly relevant because both of these prophets raise people from the dead (1 Kings 17:7-24; 2 Kings 4:8-37).[16]

Although God uses Elijah and Elisha, Scripture makes it clear that the son of the widow at Zarephath and the Shunammite's son are raised to life only by the power of God. Elijah cries, "LORD my God, let this boy's life return to

---

[16]See also 2 Kings 13:20-21.

him!" (1 Kings 17:21), and "the LORD [hears] Elijah's cry, and the boy's life [returns] to him, and he [lives]" (1 Kings 17:22). Similarly, Elisha prays to the Lord for the boy's life to be restored. These stories emphasize that only God can give life and restore people to life after death. Furthermore, these miracles serve as "previews" inasmuch as they anticipate the greater resurrection that God's people will experience in the new creation. Finally, the Lord's taking of Elijah "up to heaven in a whirlwind" (2 Kings 2:11) provides another example of a person who walked with the Lord and was spared death. These miracles and God's taking of Elijah highlight God's commitment to fulfill his promise of victory over sin and death and emphasize that death will not have the final word.

Sadly, both Israel and Judah persist in sin and rebellion, and this leads to the outcome Moses warned and prophesied about: the exile. Eventually, both the northern and southern kingdoms are defeated and taken into exile, the northern kingdom by Assyria in 722 BC, and the southern kingdom by Babylon in 587–586 BC. Although God brings judgment on Israel and Judah with the exile, there is still hope. These hopes are always centered on the line of David and the Davidic dynasty, reflecting the importance of the Davidic covenant.[17] Moreover, these hopes are also always connected with the creation themes we have traced—a renewed relationship with God, God's presence, reigning with God, and resurrection life. Significantly, when the Old Testament prophets and writers speak and write about these future hopes, they envision an even greater realization of these realities than that experienced in the old covenant.

Although there is continuity between the Old Testament and the New Testament, or the old covenant and the new covenant, there are some important differences. The old covenant represents God's promises, prophecies, and pictures of redemption. The technical term for the third descriptor is *typology*, but I often use the word *picture* because of the alliterative effect. In his description of typology, Bruce Waltke writes, "Typology . . . [pertains] to a superior fulfillment that advances salvation history. The Bible's unique Authorship and unity . . . lays [*sic*] the basis for this eschatological typology—that

---

[17]In this way, David, as an ideal (not perfect) old-covenant king, serves as a type of Jesus Christ, the perfect and final king from the line of David.

is to say, God intended earlier persons, acts, and institutions to present a type or shadow or pattern of future greater fulfillment."[18] The old covenant represents a time of anticipation and expectation, a looking forward in redemptive history. The new covenant represents the fulfillment, realization, and reality of old-covenant promises, prophecies, and pictures.

The significance of the term *picture*, or *type*, lies in the fact it points to a greater reality. God uses the sacrificial system to provide forgiveness of sins, but animals are surely not an appropriate and efficacious atonement for human sin. God is present with his people in the tabernacle and temple, but the prophets long for a new and greater temple. David is an ideal king in many respects, but the Davidic covenant is forward-looking, and the prophets long for a great and final king from the line of David to arrive in the last days. And in the old covenant, God's purpose to defeat death and provide resurrection life is also just beginning. God has led Israel out of slavery in Egypt and into the land of promise, a place of rest and life. But like the tabernacle/temple, the Levitical sacrifices, and David's kingship, Israel's experience of life in the land is a picture and foretaste of a greater reality. And just as the prophets long for a greater temple and a final son of David, they also long for a greater experience of life. These greater realities and fulfillments come to fruition in the new covenant through the person and work of Jesus Christ.

CONCLUSION AND APPLICATION

The Pentateuch and the historical books of the Old Testament affirm that God is committed to his promise to crush the head of the serpent and bring victory to humanity. God has begun to fulfill his promise of redemption, but the old covenant represents God's promises, prophecies, and pictures (or types). A picture of a family member or a friend is meaningful, but it is meaningful because it represents something more than the picture—it represents the reality behind the picture. In a similar way, the Old Testament promises, prophecies, and pictures are meaningful, but they do not represent the reality or the final fulfillment of God's redemptive plan.

---

[18]Bruce Waltke with Charles Yu, *An Old Testament Theology: An Exegetical, Canonical, and Thematic Approach* (Grand Rapids, MI: Zondervan, 2007), 137.

Here we should reflect on God's commitment to his people and his promises. God was faithful to Abraham, and he was faithful to the nation of Israel. Over and over again, we witness God's purpose to bring life to his people and to rescue them from death. Even in the midst of the exile, Israel looks forward to the time when God will fulfill his promises of redemption. These promises of redemption are nothing less than a restored relationship with God, dwelling in God's presence, reigning with God, and resurrection life. Just as the patriarchs and saints of the Old Testament did not see or experience the final fulfillment of God's promises, but rather looked forward to it, so we also look forward to the final fulfillment of those same promises (see Heb 11:39-40). God's faithfulness to his people and his promises in the past should encourage us that he will be faithful to bring them to completion in the future.

Chapter Four

SAYINGS AND SONGS
OF LIFE AND RESURRECTION

And this life that I'm living
It will not end in death
I've got a hope
That is not in this world

PIERCE PETTIS

THE OLD TESTAMENT POETIC BOOKS have often been over-looked in biblical theology since the focus of biblical theology is on God's redemptive acts in history. Nevertheless, since these books reveal snapshots that often capture the hopes and anticipations of redemption, it is unwise to ignore them. Moreover, since the New Testament authors frequently cite the psalms as evidence of the resurrection of Jesus, an investigation of the psalms is especially important in light of the topic of this book. In this chapter, I will investigate how the poetic books of the Old Testament anticipate, foreshadow, and prophesy the hope of resurrection. Once again, the creation and redemption themes we have traced are especially relevant for understanding how these books anticipate and promise resurrection hopes. In my investigation, I will briefly discuss Job and Proverbs, but the bulk of my attention will be given to the book of Psalms, which provides much fodder for discussion of resurrection in the Old Testament.

JOB

Two passages in Job have been the subject of debate and discussion in regard to resurrection hopes.[1] In Job 14:10-14, when Job is despondent and ponders his presumed punishment from God, he wonders whether it would be possible for God to allow him to die until God's punishment has passed and then later for God to bring him to life again (Job 14:13). However, Job reckons there is more hope for a tree because it can sprout again if it is cut down (Job 14:7). Thus, the answer to Job's rhetorical question, "If a man dies, shall he live again?" is likely no. Although Job is not persuaded that God will follow through with his musings, he is nevertheless convinced that God has power over death and suggests that God is able to bring people back to life after death.

In the second passage, Job 19:25-27, Job contends,

> I know that my redeemer lives,
>> and that in the end he will stand on the earth.
> And after my skin has been destroyed,
>> yet in my flesh I will see God;
> I myself will see him
>> with my own eyes—I, and not another.
>> How my heart yearns within me!

While the precise identity of Job's "redeemer" is elusive, Job hopes for and believes in a redeemer or mediator to plead his case and vindicate him. If the destruction of Job's skin in 19:26 is a reference to his death, then Job likely envisions a face-to-face encounter and vindication before God after his death. The phrase "in my flesh" could imply bodily resurrection, but the phrase can also be translated as "apart from my flesh"[2] and could refer to some other postmortem existence and vindication before God. Regardless, this passage implies both vindication and life after death for Job. Significantly, Job implies that his relationship with God is stronger than death, and communicates that his future vindication will be evidence that he is in a right relationship with God.

---

[1] Job 33:15-30 has also received attention in discussions of resurrection, but these verses likely describe God's rescue of a person from death, rather than "after death." Nevertheless, God's rescue of a person from death often serves as a paradigm for how God rescues his people after death.
[2] See NIV text note for Job 19:26.

PROVERBS

The book of Proverbs has not received much attention in discussions of resurrection. To be sure, its genre does not make it conducive for developing systematic or biblical theologies. The book contains no passages that explicitly mention the resurrection. Nevertheless, a number of themes in Proverbs are closely connected to the biblical-theological themes we have traced. For example, there is a clear contrast in Proverbs between wisdom and folly, and between submission to God and rebellion against God. In biblical thought, wisdom is not sheer intellect, an abundance of knowledge, or even the uncanny ability to make good choices. Rather, wisdom is primarily associated with submission to the Lord and his commands. Proverbs 9:10 reads, "The fear of the Lord is the beginning of wisdom, / and knowledge of the Holy One is understanding" (see also Prov 1:7; Job 28:28; Eccles 12:13). To be wise is to trust the Lord and submit to him. By contrast, foolishness is rebellion against the Lord and the spurning of wisdom.

Embedded within the contrast of wisdom and foolishness is an unmistakable contrast between life and death. Not only is the path of the adulteress a rejection of wisdom; it also leads to death (Prov 2:18; 5:5; 7:22-27). In contrast, the righteous and upright "will live in the land" (Prov 2:20-21), and those who live by wisdom and keep God's commands will be prosperous and receive prolonged life (see also Prov 3:16, 22; 4:10, 13, 20-27; 9:11; 10:27).[3] Similarly, while the righteous attain life, the outcome for the one who pursues evil is death (Prov 11:19; 15:24). Wise teaching can turn a person from death and serve as a fountain of life (Prov 13:14), and the fear of the Lord is a fountain of life that can turn a person from death (Prov 14:27). Consequently, the ones who find wisdom find life and receive blessing from the Lord, while those who hate wisdom love death (Prov 8:35-36).

These verses show that the book of Proverbs represents something more than wise and pithy sayings. These proverbs are rooted in biblical-theological themes, which were established at creation and continue throughout

---

[3] See Daniel J. Estes, *Handbook on the Wisdom Books and Psalms* (Grand Rapids, MI: Baker Academic, 2005), who also connects wisdom, righteousness, and life on the one hand, and foolishness and death on the other hand (221-24, 254-57).

redemptive history.[4] The proverb "There is a way that appears to be right, / but in the end it leads to death" (Prov 14:12; 16:25) could almost be a commentary on the fall. What seemed like a good and reasonable decision to Adam and Eve actually brought death. In an even stronger allusion, Proverbs 3:18 reads, "She [wisdom] is a tree of life to those who take hold of her."[5] To fear the Lord and submit to him is to be in a right relationship with God and therefore also to find life.

The book of Proverbs does not explicitly mention the hope of resurrection, but it anticipates it. Its teaching is rooted in biblical-theological foundations of life and death, which are connected with submission to God and rebellion against God. In Proverbs 12:28 we read, "In the way of righteousness there is life; / along that path is immortality." Although the sense is probably better communicated by the ESV ("In the path of righteousness is life, / and in its pathway there is no death"), this verse hints that a life in relationship with God extends beyond death. Proverbs 14:32 reads, "When calamity comes, the wicked are brought down, / but even in death the righteous seek refuge in God." This proverb brings into clearer focus the notion that there is hope for God's people even after death. It is impossible to know how much the authors of Proverbs envisioned resurrection hopes, but the worldview of Proverbs is firmly rooted in the creation and redemption themes identified in Genesis 1–2. This worldview, which associates life with a relationship with God, is consistent with and even anticipates resurrection hopes.

The biblical-theological foundation of these proverbs should encourage us to reflect on our own lives. Not only is it wise to live in submission to God; this is also the path of life that God created for us. On the other hand, to spurn wisdom and reject God's authority is to live a life of foolishness that ends in death. In light of the life-giving nature of God's commands (Ps 19:7-9), we should readily recognize that love for God and submission

---

[4]See, e.g., John A. Kitchen, *Proverbs: A Mentor Commentary* (Fearn, UK: Mentor, 2006), 30-34, and Bruce K. Waltke, *The Book of Proverbs: Chapters 1–15*, The New International Commentary on the Old Testament (Grand Rapids, MI: Eerdmans, 2004), 63-133. Both Kitchen and Waltke emphasize that Proverbs is a theological work that is closely linked with the theology of the entire Old Testament.

[5]See Prov 11:30, 13:12, and 15:4 for more "tree of life" references.

to his commands are the path of life. We receive foretastes of God's life-giving purposes now, but we will experience the consummation of God's life-giving purposes only in the new creation.

PSALMS

I love the psalms because many of them provide comfort for God's people. In many cases, the psalmists write about God's deliverance in the midst of difficulty, suffering, or trial. This conviction that God could rescue his people led the psalmists (and other biblical writers) to consider that God's deliverance of his people is not for this life alone but also extends beyond death. In his song "I've Got a Hope," Pierce Pettis sings of the hope that this life will not ultimately end in death. This is the same hope the psalmists on many occasions sing about and celebrate.

Martin Luther wrote that the books of Psalms "might well be called a little Bible" because "in it is comprehended most beautifully and briefly everything that is in the entire Bible." Luther continues, "I have a notion that the Holy Spirit wanted to take the trouble himself to compile a short Bible . . . so that anyone who could not read the whole Bible would here have anyway almost an entire summary of it, comprised in one little book."[6] The book of Psalms serves as the "little Bible" because the psalms provide a summary of the major themes of Scripture. All the major themes in Scripture—creation, sin, judgment, relationship with God, redemption, the kingdom of God, covenants, salvation, forgiveness, blessing, temple, God's presence, God's sovereignty, God's love, and God's mercy—are found in the psalms. Consequently, it should not come as a surprise that the psalms include resurrection hopes. These hopes at times are implicit and in seed form, and at other times are more explicit. In this section, I will investigate several psalms that anticipate resurrection hopes. In all of these psalms, the resurrection hopes are clearly connected with the themes we have traced (God's relationship with his people, God's presence, and the kingdom of God). Significantly, many

---

[6]Martin Luther, "Preface to the Psalter," in *Luther's Works*, vol. 35, *Word and Sacrament I*, ed. E. Theodore Bachmann (Philadelphia: Muhlenberg, 1960), 254.

of these psalms are cited by various New Testament authors as evidence for Jesus' resurrection.[7]

God's relationship with his people and God's life-giving presence (Ps 104, 16, 49, 73). In Psalm 104 the psalmist praises God for his wisdom and power in creation and providence. Even the creatures of the earth are ultimately dependent on God, because he is the one who provides their food and satisfies them (Ps 104:27-28). When God hides his face, they are terrified. When God takes away their breath, they die and return to the dust (Ps 104:29). When God sends his Spirit, they are created and there is renewal (Ps 104:30).

Psalm 104:27-30 is not about resurrection, but the verses highlight some foundational truths of creation, fall, and redemption. On the one hand, God's hiding his face from and taking the breath of his creatures leads to terror and death. To be cast out of God's presence and apart from God's blessing is indeed terrifying (Ps 102:2; Deut 31:17). The language of God taking the breath of his creatures and the creatures returning to dust is reminiscent of Genesis 3:19 when the Lord promises that, as a result of sin, humanity will return to the ground and the dust. On the other hand, when the psalmist reflects on God sending his Spirit, creation, and renewal (104:30), the language is reminiscent of Genesis 2:7 when "the LORD God formed a man from the dust of the ground and breathed into his nostrils the breath of life, and the man became a living being." In both Genesis 3:19 and Psalm 104:30, the life-animating power of God's Spirit is evident. As we peek forward in redemptive history, we see that God's Spirit, in addition to being the source of creation life, is the source for new-creation life and resurrection life (Ezek 37:1-14). Psalm 104:27-30 continues the trajectory that was established in creation and is carried forward in redemption: God is the giver and sustainer of life, and life is closely linked to a right relationship with him and God's presence.

Psalm 16 is also significant for the study of resurrection in the Old Testament. In this psalm, which is best understood as a psalm of confidence, David rejoices because of his security in his relationship with God. He proclaims,

---

[7]In the same passage cited above, Luther emphasizes that the Psalter also promises the death and resurrection of Christ ("Preface to the Psalter," 254).

> You will not abandon me to the realm of the dead,
>> nor will you let your faithful one see decay.
> You make known to me the path of life;
>> you will fill me with joy in your presence,
>> with eternal pleasures at your right hand. (Ps 16:10-11)

Here David is confident that God will not abandon him to "the realm of the dead."

"The realm of the dead" in the NIV translates the word *Sheol* in the Hebrew Scriptures. The Hebrew concept of Sheol is significant because it represents the place of the dead for all people—all people go to Sheol. Accordingly, Sheol is sometimes portrayed as "the great equalizer" in the Old Testament, since all people, rich and poor, strong and weak, righteous and wicked, ultimately go there.[8] Although not a place of punishment, Sheol is associated with God's judgment, since death is the consequence of sin.[9] As the biblical doctrine of resurrection unfolds, texts such as Psalm 16 (v. 10) and Psalm 49 (v. 15) reveal that God's people often possess the hope that God would deliver and redeem them from Sheol.

Although in Psalm 16 David is confident first and foremost that God will deliver him from his present perils and from a premature death (i.e., not dying at this point in his life), the language is also suggestive of a reality that extends beyond death. Richard Belcher writes,

> Some try to limit the statements of verses 9-11 to the immediate crisis the psalmist is facing. Deliverance, in this view, is from the immediate threat of death, and restoration takes place in this life. However, the language of the psalm presses toward an unbroken fellowship with the Lord beyond this life. . . . Certainly this includes more than deliverance from death in this life. There is expressed here a confident hope beyond this life and beyond the grave. Thus the path of life in verse 11 refers to eternal life, which is re-inforced by *fullness* of joy in God's presence and pleasures forevermore at his hand.[10]

---

[8]"Sheol," in *The Baker Illustrated Bible Dictionary*, ed. Tremper Longman (Grand Rapids, MI: Baker Books, 2013), 1520.

[9]"Sheol," 1520.

[10]Richard P. Belcher Jr., *The Messiah and the Psalms: Preaching Christ from All the Psalms* (Glasgow: Mentor, 2006), 164. Emphasis original.

If this is the case, David's hope was not merely that God would deliver him from a premature death but also that his relationship with God would extend beyond death. Moreover, since the "path of life" is linked with "joy in [God's] presence" and "eternal pleasures at [God's] right hand" (Ps 16:11), this experience of life after death is connected with God's presence. In this way, Psalm 16 continues the redemptive trajectory that life is the result of a right relationship with God, that God's relationship with his people extends beyond death, and that life is found in God's presence.

In addition to celebrating God's relationship with his people and God's life-giving presence, Psalm 16 is clearly linked with David's kingship. As God's anointed king, David is confident that God will not abandon him to death but will instead lead him in the path of life. As noted above, David's hope likely extended to a reality beyond death. In light of the Davidic covenant (2 Sam 7), David understood that God's covenantal promises to him were applicable for future and even greater kings from his line. In this sense, God's work, grace, and power in the life of David become a paradigm for his work in future kings in the Davidic dynasty. Peter, drawing on this psalm, proclaims that David was a prophet and spoke of the resurrection and enthronement of the Messiah in Psalm 16:8-11 (Acts 2:25-31; see also Acts 13:35). In this way, David himself and the New Testament community understood that God's promises for David and God's work in him were a paradigm for the great and final son of David, Jesus Christ.

Psalm 49 provides the most explicit Old Testament evidence for resurrection hopes to this point. The psalm contrasts the rich who trust in themselves with the upright who trust in God. Even though the psalmist suffers oppression at the hands of the rich, he knows he has nothing to fear (Ps 49:5-6). Similar to the wisdom tradition in Ecclesiastes, the psalmist recognizes that both the rich and the poor, the wise and the unwise are destined for death and the grave (Ps 49:7-12). As he wrestles with the inevitability of death and humanity's impotence to prevent it, he writes,

> No one can redeem the life of another
>   or give to God a ransom for them—
> the ransom for a life is costly,
>   no payment is ever enough—

so that they should live on forever
and not see decay. (Ps 49:7-9)

As he reflects on the foolish, he asserts that their graves will be their homes, they are "destined to die" ("appointed for Sheol" [NASB 1995]), and death will rule over them (Ps 49:11-14).

In contrast to the foolish and those who trust in themselves, the psalmist writes, "But God will redeem me from the realm of the dead; / he will surely take me to himself" (Ps 49:15). Although humanity is helpless in the face of death, God redeems from death (Sheol) and takes his people to him. God's power to redeem his people from death is precisely what gives hope to the psalmist in the face of oppression. In his commentary Allen Ross writes, "This psalm [Ps 49] is one of many in the Old Testament that express the confidence of believers in the continual, uninterrupted communion with God, i.e., the strong belief in eternal life with God. How much the psalmist actually understood is unclear, but the words convey the idea of a hope that contrasts with the death and descent of the wicked to an unseen world."[11] As Ross notes, it is impossible to discern the psalmist's precise understanding, but the psalmist expresses confidence that God will redeem his life from the power of the grave to communion with him. Moreover, the language "[God] will surely take me to himself" is similar to Genesis 5:24, where Enoch is "taken," and 2 Kings 2:1-10, where Elijah is "taken" to heaven.[12] The psalmist's hope, then, is not only that God would redeem him from death but also that God would take him to himself (Ps 49:15). Thus, Psalm 49 continues the redemptive trajectory that resurrection life is the result of a right relationship with God and that life is found in God's presence.

The psalmist of Psalm 73 faces an existential crisis of faith when he wrestles with the prosperity of the wicked in contrast to his own oppression. So great is his struggle that he proclaims,

Surely in vain I have kept my heart pure
and have washed my hands in innocence.

---

[11]Allen P. Ross, *A Commentary on the Psalms*, vol. 2, *42–89*, Kregel Exegetical Library (Grand Rapids, MI: Kregel, 2011), 157. N. T. Wright also contends that Ps 49 provides "at least a glimmer of assurance of God's ransoming power being stronger than death itself." *The Resurrection of the Son of God* (Minneapolis: Fortress, 2003), 107.

[12]See Allan Harman, *Psalms*, vol. 1, *Psalms 1–72* (Fearn, UK: Mentor, 2011), 387; Ross, *Psalms*, 2:157.

All day long I have been afflicted,
>   and every morning brings new punishments. (Ps 73:13-14)

The turning point of Psalm 73 occurs when the psalmist enters the sanctuary of God (Ps 73:17) and realizes that the apparent prosperity of the wicked is only temporary and that the fate of the wicked is destruction. In contrast to their plight, he affirms,

Yet I am always with you;
>   you hold me by my right hand.
You guide me with your counsel,
>   and afterward you will take me into glory.
Whom have I in heaven but you?
>   And earth has nothing I desire besides you.
My flesh and my heart may fail,
>   but God is the strength of my heart
>   and my portion forever. (Ps 73:23-26)

Although there are a number of interpretive difficulties (namely, whether the psalmist's experience of God's presence and glory is for this life alone or also for the life to come),[13] the psalm nevertheless describes the strong bond between God and his people and the hope of experiencing life in God's presence. Since God is "always" with the psalmist, it is possible that he envisioned a bond that was unbreakable by death and an eternal glory in God's presence.[14] Perhaps this view provides the most fitting contrast between the temporary prosperity of the wicked in this life and their eventual destruction on the one hand and the future glory for God's people on the other.[15]

In the midst of trials, the psalmists found comfort and encouragement in their relationship with God. How often do we take this relationship for granted? How often do we become overwhelmed with the difficulties and injustices of this life? These four psalms emphasize that a relationship with God is not trivial or something to be taken for granted. God is able to rescue his people from trouble and distress in this life, and God will ultimately

---

[13]See the discussion of Ross, *Psalms*, 2:569-72.
[14]See the discussions of Wright, *Resurrection*, 105-7; Belcher, *Messiah and the Psalms*, 93-97; Ross, *Psalms*, 2:569-73.
[15]See Ross, *Psalms*, 2:570.

and finally rescue his people from death in the future. As the rest of Scripture attests, the ultimate hope for believers in not in this life but in the life to come. These psalms testify to the significance of a relationship with God and anticipate that this relationship will extend beyond death in God's glorious presence.

Psalms of vindication, resurrection, and enthronement (Ps 22, 2, 110). In this section, I will discuss three psalms that anticipate the resurrection of Jesus Christ. The complicating factor is that these psalms do not explicitly teach the resurrection of believers or the resurrection of the coming Messiah. In line with the aims of biblical theology, my goal is to discuss how the hope of resurrection organically unfolds in Scripture and redemptive history. One of the challenges is to allow the Old Testament to speak on its own terms rather than reading too much of the New Testament into it. In the remainder of this chapter, I will discuss the significance of these three psalms in their Old Testament context and identify how they continue the redemptive trajectory established in Genesis 1–3. In chapter seven, I will highlight how the New Testament community and writers applied these psalms to Jesus' resurrection.

Psalm 22, a psalm of suffering and vindication, is fascinating because Jesus himself takes up the first line of the psalm on the cross (Mt 27:46; Mk 15:34) and because various New Testament authors quote and allude to the psalm to demonstrate fulfillment in Jesus Christ. In its Old Testament context, David, as a righteous and innocent sufferer, recalls a time of suffering, persecution, and despondency. David's despair is so great that he cries out,

> My God, my God, why have you forsaken me?
> > Why are you so far from saving me,
> > so far from my cries of anguish?
> My God, I cry out by day, but you do not answer,
> > by night, but I find no rest. (Ps 22:1-2)

In light of his suffering and seemingly hopeless situation, David queries whether the Lord has abandoned him.

The psalm begins as an extended lament in which David reflects on his sufferings as well as the Lord's past deliverances (Ps 22:1-18). Next, David petitions the Lord to rescue him from his adversaries and deliver him from impending death (Ps 22:19-21). The psalm ends with David's praise and vows to the Lord because of the Lord's deliverance (Ps 22:22-31). This final section is highly significant because it reveals that God has not ultimately abandoned him. On the contrary, the Lord has not despised his suffering, has not hidden his face from him,[16] but has listened (and delivered) when he cried out to God (Ps 22:24). In his celebration of God's deliverance and vindication, David declares that the ends of the earth will remember and turn to the Lord, that all the families of the nations will bow down before God, that God rules over the nations, and that the Lord will accomplish his purposes (Ps 22:27-31).

A major theme of the book of Psalms is God's faithfulness to deliver his people. This key truth is so important that the psalmists are confounded, confused, and upset when they experience God's lack of deliverance. This is the source of David's angst in Psalm 22. But taken in its entirety, Psalm 22 emphasizes that God has not ultimately abandoned David in the midst of his suffering. On the contrary, God has vindicated him, even in the midst of the threat of death. This example from David's life serves as a paradigm for God's faithfulness to all his people. Even though believers experience trials and tribulations, even to the point of feeling that God might have abandoned them, God never abandons his people, and he is always with them.

In the light of God's covenant with David, there is a heightened sense in which the psalm applies to David and the kings that come from his line. God has promised that he will never take his love from David and that his throne will be established forever (2 Sam 7:14-16). In this sense, Psalm 22 is a paradigm for the future kings that will come from the line of David.

The New Testament writers contend that Psalm 22 is fulfilled in Jesus Christ, the final and ultimate king from the line of David. They frequently cite Psalm 22 for Jesus' suffering and his death on the cross.[17] But if David's suffering in Psalm 22 anticipates the suffering of the future messianic king, there is reason to believe that David's deliverance and vindication in Psalm 22 also anticipates Jesus' vindication and deliverance. Not only is the suffering

---

[16]The reference in Ps 22:24 to God not hiding his face from David emphasizes that God has not withheld his life-giving presence and blessing.

[17]See, e.g., Mt 27:46; 27:39; 27:43; Jn 19:28; 19:23-24.

heightened for the final son of David, so also is the deliverance heightened for the final son of David. Whereas David was vindicated and delivered from death, Jesus is vindicated by God and delivered after death through resurrection. This is a theme we will explore in chapter seven in our discussion of Jesus' resurrection from the dead.[18]

Psalm 2 is a royal psalm, and the theme of kingship permeates the psalm.[19] While many psalms emphasize either God's heavenly reign or the reign of the earthly king, Psalm 2 celebrates both realities—God's heavenly kingship and the earthly kingship of the Lord's anointed one, who is appointed by the Lord to accomplish his purposes on earth. Although the psalm has no title, the New Testament clarifies that David was the author (Acts 4:25-26) and most likely the original referent. In light of the Lord's decree in Psalm 2:7 ("You are my son; / today I have become your father"), an almost certain allusion to 2 Samuel 7:14, David most likely wrote the psalm to reflect on his coronation and God's promises to him in 2 Samuel 7.

The basic structure of Psalm 2 summarizes the flow and content of the passage. In the first three verses, David identifies the problem: the rebellion of the nations against the Lord and his anointed king. In Psalm 2:4-6 God responds to the rebellion of the nations with the installation and enthronement of his king. The Lord, the one who sits in the heavens, laughs and even scoffs because this rebellion is no match for his heavenly reign and his earthly king. In the third section (Ps 2:7-9), the Lord declares that David is his "son," and gives an astounding offer to the son: the nations of the world as his inheritance and the ends of the earth as his possession. In the final section (Ps 2:10-12), God gives an invitation and word of warning to the kings of the earth and the nations of the world. They can serve the Lord and submit to the son to receive blessing, or they can continue in their rebellion and suffer God's wrath.

---

[18]Ps 31 is another example of a psalm in which Jesus quotes some of the words when he is on the cross ("Into your hands I commit my spirit" [Ps 31:5; Lk 23:46]). In the psalm, David entrusts himself to God's care and protection, asks for deliverance, and is delivered from death by God. In this way, Ps 31 serves as a similar paradigm for Jesus' death and resurrection. Jesus commits himself to his Father's care and protection, and is delivered through death by God in his resurrection from the dead.

[19]A small portion of my discussion of Ps 2 is taken from M. Jeff Brannon, "Psalm 2 in the History of Redemption," *Biblical Perspectives* 23, no. 51 (2021), http://reformedperspectives.org/magazine/article.asp/link/http:%5E%5Ereformedperspectives.org%5Earticles%5Ejef_%20brannon%5Ejef_brannon.Psalm2.pdf/at/Psalm%202%20in%20the%20History%20of%20Redemption.

In Genesis 3:15 God promised there would be enmity between the offspring of the woman and the serpent. This enmity has been evident throughout redemptive history, from Cain's murder of Abel to the attempted genocide of Israel by Pharaoh and Egypt. The precarious situation of Psalm 2 continues this trajectory, as the kings of the world rebel against the Lord and his anointed king. Psalm 2 celebrates the answer to this hostility: God will quell the rebellion of the nations through his anointed king. It advances redemptive history through the celebration of a king from the family of Abraham, to whom God has offered the nations and the ends of the earth. At its core, Psalm 2 represents the ideals, hopes, expectations, and even the certain future of the Davidic kingdom. God will extend his reign to the ends of the earth through the installment, enthronement, and reign of his anointed king.

Although Psalm 2 is not predictive of the Messiah in its Old Testament context, because of the allusion to 2 Samuel 7 (Ps 2:7) the psalm anticipates future fulfillment and has an eschatologically oriented trajectory. This connection with 2 Samuel 7 means that Psalm 2 anticipates future and greater kings. The New Testament authors and community emphasize that Psalm 2 reaches its final fulfillment in the reign of Jesus Christ. Specifically, they point out that Jesus' resurrection from the dead and ascension into heaven represent his enthronement and formal installation as king.

Psalm 110, a royal psalm in which David prophesies about a greater priest-king, continues the theme and trajectory of kingship in redemptive history. In Genesis 1:26-33 God gives humanity the task and privilege of reigning over all creation. Psalm 8, a reflection on this original commission, says that God has put everything under humanity's feet. In Genesis 3:15 God decrees that the offspring of the woman will crush the head of the serpent. Psalm 110 alludes to these passages when the Lord (Yahweh) says to David's lord (Adonai, i.e., one greater than David),

> "Sit at my right hand
> until I make your enemies
> a footstool for your feet."

> The LORD will extend your mighty scepter from Zion, saying,
> "Rule in the midst of your enemies!" (Ps 110:1-2)

While God establishes his covenant with David and his descendants in 2 Samuel 7, Psalm 110 specifies that a future son of David will bring the eschatological kingdom, and this future king will rule over his enemies and bring judgment to the nations. Furthermore, Psalm 110 clarifies that this future son of David will reign at the right hand of God.

From its Old Testament context, ancient readers would have understood that this son of David will be exalted by God in some manner, enthroned, and imbued with power by God. As the Old Testament anticipates and as the New Testament makes explicit, this great and final son of David ushers in the eschatological kingdom of God, reigns at the right hand of God, and defeats God's enemies. As redemptive history unfolds, the prophets emphasize that the hope of resurrection is closely linked with the eschatological kingdom of God. The New Testament community stresses that Psalm 110 is fulfilled in Jesus' resurrection, ascension, and heavenly enthronement. The close connection between Jesus' resurrection and enthronement is a theme we will return to in chapter seven.

CONCLUSION AND APPLICATION

The poetic books of the Old Testament continue the trajectory established at creation and with the first promise of redemption. After the fall, God is at work to bring redemption to his people, and this redemption is nothing less than victory over death. The book of Proverbs associates life with a right relationship with God, and death with foolishness and rebellion against God. The book of Psalms provides the clearest evidence for resurrection to this point. A number of psalms teach or imply that God's relationship with his people extends beyond death, and connect this future life with God's presence. That the kingship psalms anticipate the future resurrection and reign of Jesus is established by how the New Testament writers appeal to them as evidence for Jesus' resurrection.

In times of suffering, the psalmists often turn their hearts to God, remember God's faithfulness, and endeavor to trust God for the future. They often long for God's blessing to return to their lives. As they reflect on God's faithfulness, the psalmists also at times emphasize that God's faithfulness and their relationship with the Lord will extend even beyond death. We would do well to remember and reflect on these hopes and promises. God has promised that he is with us and that he will never leave us, even to the point of death and beyond. Our ultimate hope is that God's wonderful blessing will continue for eternity, even after death—that "God will redeem [us] from the realm of the dead" and that "he will surely take [us] to himself" (Ps 49:15).

Chapter Five

PROPHECIES OF RESURRECTION

I've been looking so long at these pictures of you
that I almost believe that they're real.

THE CURE

PERHAPS NO BOOKS OF THE BIBLE are as confusing and misunderstood as the Old Testament prophetic books. I remember a time many years ago when I set out to read the prophetic books and, after getting a few chapters in, concluded, "Well, so much for that—back to the New Testament." If we are honest, this is often our experience when we attempt to read these challenging books. Here I will highlight two important themes that help us interpret and navigate the murky waters of the prophetic books: judgment and hope.[1] God brings judgment on Israel because of sin and rebellion, yet even in the midst of judgment and punishment, the prophets write about a glorious hope and future for God's people. Their hopes are centered on a renewed relationship with God, the last-days kingdom of God, life in God's presence, and the hope of resurrection. In this chapter, I will investigate the resurrection hopes and

---

[1]Vaughan Roberts identifies these two major themes of the prophetic books in *God's Big Picture: Tracing the Storyline of the Bible* (Downers Grove, IL: InterVarsity Press, 2012), 95-99.

prophecies that come into clearer focus in the Old Testament prophetic books. I will focus my attention on the passages that touch on resurrection in Hosea, Isaiah, Ezekiel, and Daniel, consistent with the likely order these books were written.

JUDGMENT

In chapter three, I briefly discussed the Davidic covenant, the united kingdom of Israel, the divided kingdom, and the eventual exile of the northern and southern kingdoms. In light of the consequences of the exile, it should not be surprising that God's judgment is directly related to the themes we have traced. First, although there is always a faithful remnant, Israel has broken God's covenant and falls under God's judgment. The prophet Jeremiah even uses the metaphor of divorce to describe God's relationship with Israel and Judah (Jer 3:6-10). Israel has broken God's covenant, and the nation's relationship with God is severed. Second, when Babylon defeats Judah, King Jehoachin is taken into captivity and there is no king from the line of David on the throne (2 Kings 24:15-20). Moreover, as Israel and Judah are taken into exile, they are not reigning over creation as God intended. Third, in the Babylonian judgment, both Jerusalem and the temple are destroyed. Since many of God's people no longer dwell in the land and since the temple is destroyed, God's people are separated from his presence.

Israel's relationship with God is broken, Israel no longer serves as God's vice-regents, and Israel is separated from God's presence. These judgments are representative of death as the consequence of sin. Just as Adam and Eve suffered a broken relationship with God, exile from God's presence, a failure to serve as God's vice-regents, and ultimately death, so now Israel has broken God's covenant and suffers the consequences of a severed relationship with God, exile from God's presence, and not reigning with God. The prophet Jeremiah's words, "Death has climbed in through our windows / and has entered our fortresses" (Jer 9:21), are a fitting description of God's judgment and the horrors of the exile.

HOPE

In addition to judgment, Moses prophesied about a time of restoration, blessing, and prosperity for God's people after exile (Deut 30:1-10). The offer for God's people is to "return to the LORD your God and obey him with all your heart and with all your soul" (Deut 30:2). No wonder Moses describes this restoration with these words:

> Even if you have been banished to the most distant land under the heavens, from there the LORD your God will gather you and bring you back. He will bring you to the land that belonged to your ancestors, and you will take possession of it. He will make you more prosperous and numerous than your ancestors. The LORD your God will circumcise your hearts and the hearts of your descendants, so that you may love him with all your heart and with all your soul, and *live*. (Deut 30:4-6, emphasis added)

With this hope, Moses envisions a restoration that would be greater than Israel's first experience of life in the land.

Like Moses, the Old Testament prophets looked forward to these future restoration hopes. This longing and expectation for the future greater blessings highlights the contrast between the old and new covenants. As discussed, the old covenant is represented by promise, prophecy, and picture (or type), while the new covenant is represented by fulfillment, realization, and reality. Although the blessings experienced under the old covenant were genuine, they were not the final fulfillment. God's blessing of life in the land was a wonderful blessing, but it pales in comparison to the life promised in the new covenant. The song "Pictures of You" by The Cure provides a reminder that pictures are not the same as the reality. Pictures are powerful and meaningful, but they are no substitute for the real thing. The same is true for the Old Testament "pictures," since they always point to something greater. In light of the glorious future that the prophets envision, they imply that the old-covenant experience of life in the land was a "picture" of the eschatological new-creation life that God intends to bring to his people.

The future and greater realities that the prophets write about are directly related to the themes we have traced. First, the prophets speak of a new covenant in which God's people are forgiven and restored to God (Jer 31:31-34;

Ezek 11:18-21). Second, they envision an end-time kingdom of righteousness and peace that the final son of David would usher in (Is 9:1-7; 11:1-16; Jer 33:14-18). Third, God promises that his people will return to the land and the place of his presence for this time of blessing and prosperity. If the restoration experiences of God's relationship with his people, the kingdom of God, and life in God's presence are greater than the old-covenant experience, it makes sense that the experience of life in the new covenant will also be greater. Resurrection hopes spring from this reality, and this serves as the subject of this chapter.[2]

HOSEA

Like all the prophetic books, Hosea's prophecies include threats of judgment and the hope of restoration. Two restoration passages in particular have provided fodder for discussion of resurrection: Hosea 6:1-2 and Hosea 13:14. In Hosea 6:1-2 we read,

> Come, let us return to the LORD.
> He has torn us to pieces
>   but he will heal us;
> he has injured us
>   but he will bind up our wounds.
> After two days he will revive us;
>   on the third day he will restore us,
>   that we may live in his presence.

In the midst of Israel's despair on account of the exile, the plea is for the nation to return to the Lord, wherein God's people will find revival, restoration, and life in God's presence. Although the passage does not explicitly teach resurrection, resurrection language and imagery are employed to describe redemptive themes that are linked to resurrection hopes.

The context of the passage is the restoration of Israel. This context is significant since Israel's experience of life in the land was merely a type of a future greater reality. The promise of Israel's return to the land actually

---

[2]On the motif of Israel's exile as a "death" and Israel's restoration as a "resurrection," see Donald E. Gowan, *Theology of the Prophetic Books: The Death and Resurrection of Israel* (Louisville, KY: Westminster John Knox, 1998).

anticipates a future and greater experience of life, a promise that is ultimately fulfilled in the resurrection life of God's people in the new creation. Moreover, the hope of life in God's presence (Hos 6:2) hints at and implies resurrection, even if the reference is not explicit.[3] The terminology of the Lord *reviving* his people is also noteworthy. Although it is impossible to know if resurrection was in view, there is an intimate connection between renewed spiritual life and resurrection. Those who have a renewed relationship with God will inherit resurrection life in the future. Finally, although the reference is figurative, perhaps for demonstrating the Lord's willingness to heal his people, Hosea proclaims that this revival and restoration will happen "on the third day" (Hos 6:2). The New Testament writers likely had this verse in mind when they claimed the Old Testament Scriptures testified to the resurrection of the Messiah on the third day.[4] This reinforces the notion that resurrection is in view in Hosea 6:1-2.

The second passage, centered on Hosea 13:14, is difficult for a number of reasons. Depending on the interpretation and translation, the verse can read one of two ways:

> Should I ransom them from the grave?
>> Should I redeem them from death?
> O death, bring on your terrors!
>> O grave, bring on your plagues!
>> For I will not take pity on them. (NLT)

> I will deliver this people from the power of the grave;
>> I will redeem them from death.
> Where, O death, are your plagues?
>> Where, O grave, is your destruction?
> I will have no compassion. (NIV)

The complicating issue is whether the words of Hosea 13:14 should be read as questions ("Should I ransom them from the grave? / Should I redeem them from death?" [NLT]) or as statements ("I will deliver this people from the

---

[3]The hope for life in God's presence in Hos 6:1-2 is similar to David's expectation in Ps 16:10-11.
[4]See Jesus' statement in Lk 24:46 and the curious and perplexed reaction of Jesus' disciples in Lk 24:21.

power of the grave; / I will redeem them from death" [NIV]). Taking into account the judgment context, the first translation (NLT) emphasizes that God will not ransom his people from Sheol or redeem them from death.[5] In this view, the subsequent statements of Hosea 13:14 ("O death, bring on your terrors! / O grave, bring on your plagues!" [NLT]) represent the weapons of death that God will use to punish rebellious Israel.[6]

In the latter translation (NIV), God promises redemption from death, providing hope in the midst of judgment and anticipating the restoration of Hosea 14. In this view, the questions of Hosea 13:14 represent God's taunting death and the grave because he has redeemed his people from death through resurrection life. Such a contrast between judgment and hope is not inconsistent with other prophetic oracles as these two themes are routinely interwoven in the prophetic books. Moreover, Paul's quotation of Hosea 13:14 in 1 Corinthians 15:55 carries this positive sense—that God will ransom his people from the power of the grave and redeem them from death.

In light of the judgment context, the NLT translation and interpretation are likely correct. On account of their sin and rebellion, God promises that he will punish Israel and not deliver them from death. But we should not miss God's call for Israel to repent and turn to him for blessing in Hosea 14. The implication is that God will certainly follow through with the judgment of Hosea 13:14 if his people do not repent. However, if his people repent, they will find forgiveness, healing, blessing, flourishing (Hos 14:1-9), and, by implication, deliverance and redemption from death and the grave (Hos 13:14). While the context of Hosea 13:14 is judgment, the hope of restoration, forgiveness, and resurrection comes through repentance.

Regardless of the interpretation of Hosea 13:14, the verse is significant for a number of reasons. First, only God has power over death, and only God can redeem people from the grave. Moreover, there is a clear contrast between those who are in a right relationship with God and those in rebellion against God. Whether directly or indirectly, God promises that he will redeem his

---

[5]See also the NASB and NRSV for this interpretation and translation.

[6]These subsequent statements are questions in Hebrew, and are usually translated as questions (see, e.g., NASB, NRSV, NIV, ESV). The NLT's translation of them into statements emphasizes God's determination to punish his people through death.

people (those in a restored relationship with God) from death. By contrast, those in rebellion against God can expect only judgment and death. In this way, Hosea 13:14 implies that death will not have the final say and that death will not retain its sting and power for God's people.[7]

ISAIAH

Once, when I was teaching an Old Testament class, I wanted to make the point that the prophetic books are difficult, confusing, and unfamiliar. Much to my dismay, one student was convinced that they were "memorable." When I objected, he began to rattle off passage after passage from Isaiah that was "memorable" or "meaningful" to him. To his point, the book of Isaiah is probably the most familiar of the prophetic books, save for the possible exception of Jonah. Isaiah's encounter with the Lord (Is 6); the famous "Christmas" passage (Is 9); the famous, "Surely the nations are like a drop in a bucket" line (Is 40:15), which is quoted in the movie *Chariots of Fire*; soaring on wings like eagles (Is 40:28-31); passing through the waters (Is 43:1-3); and the suffering servant (Is 52:13–53:12) are indeed memorable. Although some famous lines or passages might be familiar, the reality is that the book of Isaiah, like all the prophetic books, is challenging to interpret. The themes of judgment and hope provide a helpful orientation for understanding the book.

Prophecies of resurrection (Is 25–26). Isaiah 13–27 records God's proclamations of judgment against various nations, including Israel. Toward the end of the oracles, Isaiah speaks of Israel's restoration, and two passages in particular are significant since they include resurrection hopes: 25:6-9 and 26:19.

In Isaiah 25:7-8, Isaiah prophesies,

> On this mountain he will destroy
>   the shroud that enfolds all peoples,
> the sheet that covers all nations;
>   he will swallow up death forever.

---

[7]In 1 Cor 15:55, on account of Christ's resurrection, Paul quotes Hos 13:14 to celebrate this reality—that death no longer retains its sting, power, and victory. Because Jesus has overcome sin and death in his resurrection, those united to him will also overcome sin and death through resurrection.

> The Sovereign LORD will wipe away the tears
>> from all faces;
> he will remove his people's disgrace
>> from all the earth.

Isaiah's prophecy is significant for our purpose to trace the unfolding hope of resurrection. On the one hand, God's swallowing up of death forever is explicitly connected with salvation. The response of God's people to the Lord's work is

> Surely this is our God;
>> we trusted in him, and he saved us.
> This is the LORD, we trusted in him;
>> let us rejoice and be glad in his salvation. (Is 25:9)

The prophecy emphasizes that God's salvation of his people is incomplete without death being conquered. Accompanying God's swallowing up of death is the promise that God will wipe the tears from his people and remove their disgrace (Is 25:8). The great curse of sin is death. No other curse in history has caused so much pain, turmoil, tears, and disgrace. Here God promises that he will tenderly wipe the tears from his people and that he will, once and for all, remove the disgrace of his people.

Although Isaiah 25:6-9 does not explicitly teach resurrection,[8] the implication is so strong that Paul alludes to Isaiah 25:8 in his argument for resurrection when he proclaims, "Death has been swallowed up in victory" (1 Cor 15:54). God's promise that the offspring of the woman will crush the head of the serpent implies and guarantees that death, as the curse of sin, will be undone. These verses continue that trajectory and identify redemption with God's swallowing up death and removing the curse of death from his people.

In the midst of his oracles, Isaiah emphasizes that the kings who oppressed and ruled over Israel are now dead and their spirits do not rise (Is 26:13-14). In contrast to their fate, Isaiah writes of Israel and Judah,

---

[8]See the discussion of Lidija Novakovic, *Raised from the Dead According to Scripture: The Role of Israel's Scripture in the Early Christian Interpretations of Jesus' Resurrection* (London: Bloomsbury, 2012), 74-76. Novakovic notes that although the passage does not mention resurrection, it describes the joy of those who witness the reversal of the curse of death (75).

But your dead will live, LORD;
  their bodies will rise—
let those who dwell in the dust
  wake up and shout for joy—
your dew is like the dew of the morning;
  the earth will give birth to her dead. (Is 26:19)

While some scholars understand this promise of resurrection as metaphorical, there are at least two reasons to understand Isaiah 26:19 as an actual description of future bodily resurrection. First, the contrast between God's people who will be raised to life and the oppressive kings and nations whose fate is death (Is 26:13-14) suggests bodily resurrection. Second, the emphasis on cosmic renewal in the larger context implies physical resurrection.[9]

In the context of Isaiah 24–27, Isaiah links resurrection with Israel's restoration hopes.[10] As we have seen, the Bible often describes the land of promise as a place of "life," but this first experience of life in the land is merely a type or a foreshadowing of a greater experience to come. In line with Moses, the Old Testament prophets predict a greater experience of life with Israel's restoration to the land. Isaiah associates this greater experience of life in the land with resurrection. This is a remarkable development, but not surprising in light of the redemptive trajectory in Scripture. In the biblical story of creation and redemption, life is always connected with the place of God's presence. The resurrection promise of Isaiah 26 continues this trajectory and clarifies that God's people will be raised to new life, which will be experienced in Israel's return to the land. But just as the experience of life in the land in the old covenant is a picture of a future and greater life, so the land in the old covenant is a picture of something greater: the new creation. Seen in this light, Isaiah's prophecy will ultimately be fulfilled through resurrection life in the new creation.

The song of the suffering servant (Is 52:13–53:12). On account of the varied and ambiguous references to the "servant" in Isaiah, the Servant Songs have been the subject of much debate. At times the servant in Isaiah is

---

[9]See N. T. Wright, *The Resurrection of the Son of God* (Minneapolis: Fortress, 2003), 117.
[10]Wright closely associates Israel's national hope for restoration with resurrection; *Resurrection*, 122-28.

identified as the nation of Israel (Is 44:1; 49:3), while at other times the servant in Isaiah is identified as the person who will bring salvation to Israel and the ends of the earth (Is 50:4-11).[11] What is clear from the servant passages in Isaiah is the servant's essential role in God's plan of redemption. In Isaiah 52:13–53:12, Isaiah seems to have a singular figure in mind[12] when he prophecies about the suffering of God's servant and, as we will see, the vindication of God's servant after suffering. Three items are of significance for our investigation: the suffering of the servant and salvation for God's people, the vindication of the servant, and the servant's righteousness and vindication.

First, the song of the suffering servant connects salvation with the suffering and sacrifice of the servant. Ever since the fall, God has provided sacrifices so that his people can live. Isaiah 52:13–53:12 brings this motif into clearer focus. The sacrifice that will allow God's people to live will ultimately come not from an animal (see Heb 10:4) but from God's righteous servant. This servant will be "despised and rejected," "a man of suffering" (Is 53:3), "oppressed and afflicted" (Is 53:7), yet he will experience all of this not because of his own sin but because of the sin of his people. The servant will be "pierced for our transgressions," "crushed for our iniquities" (Is 53:5), punished for the transgression of God's people (Is 53:8), and "an offering for sin" (Is 53:10). God's people will be healed by his wounds (Is 53:5), brought peace by his punishment (Is 53:5), and justified through him (Is 53:11). In this way, the song poignantly communicates that life for God's people will come only through the sacrifice of God's righteous, suffering servant.

Second, although the servant will suffer and die, the song emphasizes that the final result for the servant is not suffering and death. An overlooked aspect of the song of the suffering servant is its beginning, in which the Lord

---

[11]This ambiguity makes sense within biblical theology, since there is a close relationship in Old and New Testament theology between the Messiah and the people of the Messiah. In the New Testament, Jesus brings salvation to his people, but God also uses believers to bring salvation to the ends of the earth. In this vein, while Jesus is clearly identified as the servant of Is 42 (see, e.g., Lk 4:21), Jesus also commissions Paul to open the eyes of the Gentiles, turn them from darkness to light, and turn them from the power of Satan to God (Acts 26:17-18), a clear reference to the servant in Is 42:6-7.

[12]A singular figure who suffers on behalf of the nation is the natural reading of the passage, although it should be noted that the dominant interpretation before Jesus held that the servant was a reference to the nation of Israel.

proclaims, "See, my servant will act wisely; / he will be raised and lifted up and highly exalted" (Is 52:13). In light of this unusual beginning for a song that emphasizes suffering, many scholars correctly recognize that the passage "begins with the ending."[13] In its Old Testament context, it is difficult to know precisely what Isaiah envisions with the language of "raised and lifted up and highly exalted," but the verse clearly communicates vindication and exaltation for the servant.

Forming a bookend with the beginning, the end of the song (Is 53:10-12) is significant since it also emphasizes the vindication and exaltation of the servant. In Isaiah 53:10-11 we read,

> Yet it was the LORD's will to crush him and cause him to suffer,
>> and though the LORD makes his life an offering for sin,
> he will see his offspring and prolong his days,
>> and the will of the LORD will prosper in his hand.
> After he has suffered,
>> he will see the light of life and be satisfied.

Although the servant suffers, the end of the song speaks of his vindication. Although the term *resurrection* does not appear, the verses imply that the servant will experience life[14] after he has suffered and given himself as an offering for sin.[15] In light of the promise of life after death, it is reasonable to conclude that his vindication comes through resurrection. In Isaiah 53:12 the Lord declares, "Therefore I will give him a portion among the great, / and he will divide the spoils with the strong." In addition to resurrection, this suggests exaltation and victory for the servant. Within the song, the journey of the servant is from death to life (Is 53:9-10), from condemnation to righteousness (Is 53:8, 11), and from helplessness to victory (Is 53:7, 12).[16] This

---

[13]See the discussion of Andrew M. Davis, *Exalting Jesus in Isaiah*, Christ-Centered Exposition Commentary (Nashville: Holman, 2017), 318-19.

[14]The phrase "the light of life" is in the Dead Sea Scrolls but not in the Masoretic Text. Regardless of whether the phrase should be included, J. Alex Motyer argues that the Masoretic Text implies the meaning; see *The Prophecy of Isaiah: An Introduction and Commentary* (Downers Grove, IL: IVP Academic, 1993), 441n2.

[15]See J. Alex Motyer, *Isaiah*, Tyndale Old Testament Commentary 20 (Downers Grove, IL: Inter-Varsity Press, 1999), 381.

[16]Motyer, *Isaiah*, 381.

journey suggests that vindication, resurrection, and exaltation, rather than suffering and death, are the final result for the servant.

Third, there is a direct correlation between the righteousness of the suffering servant and vindication, justification, and life. The servant "acts wisely" (Is 52:13), has done no violence, has no deceit, and is "righteous" (Is 53:9-12). On the one hand, the righteousness of the servant is intimately connected with his own vindication, resurrection, and exaltation (Is 53:10-12). On the other hand, the sacrifice and righteousness of the suffering servant is also the source of life and justification for others. In Isaiah 53:5 the servant is "pierced for our transgressions" and "crushed for our iniquities," and it is his punishment that brings peace, healing, and life for God's people. As Isaiah 53:11 communicates, this righteous servant "will justify many." Consequently, the righteousness of the suffering servant is the basis for his own vindication, and his righteousness and vindication are the basis for the vindication of his people. These themes, the connection between life and a right relationship with God on the one hand and substitutionary atonement on the other hand, take us back to Genesis 1–3, yet also propel us forward to the true servant of God—the Lord Jesus Christ—who will give his life as an atonement for sin, who will be vindicated because of his righteousness, and whose vindication will serve as the source of vindication for his people.

EZEKIEL

At the heart of Ezekiel's restoration hopes are the eschatological kingdom of God, a return to the land, a restored temple, and a restored Jerusalem. Perhaps Ezekiel's most famous restoration passage is chapter 37. The chapter can be divided into two passages: the valley of dry bones (Ezek 37:1-14) and the eschatological kingdom (Ezek 37:15-28). In the first passage, God calls Ezekiel to prophesy to dead bones, and promises that breath will enter the bones and they will come to life (Ezek 37:4-9). At Ezekiel's prophecy, the bones come to life and stand on their feet (Ezek 37:10). In Ezekiel 37:11 God clarifies that the bones represent the whole house of Israel, whose hope is gone and who are cut off, no doubt on account of the exile. The vision ends with God's declaration: "My people, I am going to open your graves and bring you up from them; I will bring you back to the land of Israel. Then you, my people,

will know that I am the LORD, when I open your graves and bring you up
from them. I will put my Spirit in you and you will live, and I will settle you
in your own land" (Ezek 37:12-14).

Although scholars debate the vision's meaning, the resurrection images
are striking. On the one hand, the connection between the word of the Lord
and breath entering dead bones finds its background in creation. Just as God
spoke creation into existence and breathed life into Adam, here in Ezekiel
God's prophetic word and his breath are instrumental in the bones coming
to life. This suggests that a new creation is in view in Ezekiel 37:4-10. On the
other hand, God's promise that he will open the graves of his people and
bring them up from their graves is a graphic resurrection image. At face value,
it does not seem unreasonable to conclude that Ezekiel envisions a future
bodily resurrection for God's people. Nevertheless, many scholars have interpreted these images primarily as the restoration of Israel coming from
exile and secondarily as a spiritual awakening of God's people.[17]

In light of the Lord's explanation (Ezek 37:11-14), the vision is indeed a
metaphor for the national restoration of Israel and the spiritual renewal that
will accompany this restoration. However, Ezekiel's use of resurrection language to describe this restoration is significant. N. T. Wright notes the connection between Israel's restoration and resurrection when he writes, "Where
a strong sense of exile as divine punishment for rebellion, disloyalty and
idolatry was present . . . , then it was but a short step for that expulsion to be
seen as 'death,' life in exile to be seen as the strange half-life lived after that
death, and return from exile to be seen as life beyond that again, newly
embodied life, i.e. resurrection."[18] The question before us is why there is a
close connection between Israel's restoration hopes and resurrection. In my
estimation, the close relationship between the themes we have traced makes
sense of this connection. As we have seen, the land represented both the
place of God's presence and a place of life for God's people. A return to the

---

[17]For many scholars, the resurrection language describes the national and spiritual restoration of
Israel, but the language is picked up by later writers (e.g., Daniel) to argue for future bodily resurrection. See, e.g., Novakovic, *Raised from the Dead*, 73, and Wright, *Resurrection*, 119-21.

[18]Wright, *Resurrection*, 122. See Wright's discussion in *Resurrection*, 122-28. Gowan (*Theology of
the Prophetic Books*, 9) describes the exile and restoration of Israel as "the death and resurrection
of Israel" and identifies Ezek 37:1-14 as a key text for this motif.

land represents a return to God's presence and therefore also a return to life in God's presence. The restoration experience after the exile was to be a greater experience of life. In this sense, the promise of restoration for Israel anticipates a greater life to come—and the prophets recognized that this was nothing less than resurrection life.

God's promises in Ezekiel 36:26-27 that he will give his people a new heart and put a new spirit in them, that he will remove their heart of stone and give them a heart of flesh, and that he will place his Spirit in them to follow his decrees and keep his laws demonstrate that there is good reason indeed to understand Ezekiel's vision of the valley of dry bones as the spiritual awakening of God's people. Throughout redemptive history, a right relationship with God is always associated with life. In this vein, the spiritual (i.e., of the Holy Spirit) rebirth of Ezekiel 37 actually implies and culminates in an eschatological physical resurrection. G. K. Beale contends, "The parallelism with Ezek. 36 indicates that the prophecy of Israel's resurrection in Ezek. 37 does indicate new creation, but in terms of resurrection of the spirit. And resurrection of the spirit is inextricably linked to resurrection of the body, the latter of which is how the majority of Judaism understood the Ezek. 37 prophecy."[19] Thus, the biblical pattern is that God gives new spiritual life to his people and this new spiritual life culminates in bodily resurrection. In light of this, the resurrection language of Ezekiel 37 is both understandable and appropriate.

Ezekiel 37:1-14 connects Israel's return to the land and the promise of spiritual renewal with the hope of resurrection. The next passage (Ezek 37:15-28) links Israel's restoration hopes with a restored relationship with God, God's presence, and the eschatological kingdom of God. First, in reference to a restored relationship with God, the Lord promises that his people will no longer defile themselves with idols, he will save his people from their sinful backsliding, he will cleanse them, and he will be their God and they his people (Ezek 37:23). Significantly, God also promises that he will make an everlasting covenant of peace with his people (Ezek 37:26). In light of Ezekiel 36:25-29, this covenant is explicitly connected with the eschatological pouring out of

---

[19]G. K. Beale, *A New Testament Biblical Theology: The Unfolding of the Old Testament in the New* (Grand Rapids, MI: Baker Academic, 2011), 230.

God's Spirit and a new heart. Second, in reference to God's presence, God promises that he will put his sanctuary among his people forever and that his dwelling place will be with them (Ezek 37:26-28). In the new covenant, this is fulfilled by God's Spirit indwelling his people (Ezek 36:26-27) and by the return of God's people to the land (Ezek 36:33-36; 37:12-14). Third, in reference to the kingdom, God promises that there will no longer be two nations, but rather one nation and one kingdom, and one king who rules over his people. This eschatological king is God's servant from the line of David (Ezek 37:22, 24).

The hope of resurrection, although not explicit in Ezekiel 37:15-28, is strongly implied. In light of Ezekiel's emphasis on a restored relationship with God, a return to the place of God's presence, and the eschatological kingdom of God, it should not be surprising that resurrection hopes also come into focus, since life and resurrection are always closely linked with these other realities. God promises that his people "will live in the land" and that they and their descendants "will live there forever" (Ezek 37:25). The motif of life in the land is a picture of a greater reality and fulfillment to come. Accordingly, God's promise that his people "will live in the land" will ultimately be fulfilled through resurrection life in the new creation. This conclusion finds further confirmation from Ezekiel 36:35, where we read, "This land that was laid waste has become like the garden of Eden." In this verse, the redemptive trajectory from the garden to the land and finally to the new creation comes into focus. The Garden of Eden is the paradigm for creation life, the land of promise is a picture and foreshadowing of a greater life to come, and the new creation is the final fulfillment of this promise of eschatological life. This future eschatological life is something akin to a return to Eden, but in light of God's promises, the experience of resurrection life in the new creation will be greater even than the original Eden.

The first preaching of the gospel promised that the offspring of the woman would crush the head of the serpent. This entails nothing less than a restored relationship with God, reigning with God, a return to life in God's presence, and resurrection life. A remarkable chapter, Ezekiel 37 brings together these redemptive hopes and demonstrates how closely linked they are. Regardless of whether Ezekiel envisioned bodily resurrection, resurrection is implied and anticipated by a return to the land as the place of God's presence, a renewed relationship with God, and the promise of the eschatological kingdom. In my view, there is good reason to conclude that Ezekiel actually connected resurrection with these other restoration hopes. Consequently, it should not come as a surprise to find resurrection language in Ezekiel 37. Indeed, for this passage, which looks to the distant future, to be of any meaningful hope for the original audience, resurrection must be in view. The eschatological hopes of Ezekiel 37:24-28, which include the future reign of the great son of David, a new covenant, and God dwelling with his people, confirm that the restoration promises of Ezekiel 37 culminate in a new creation, and essential to these eschatological hopes is resurrection from the dead.

DANIEL

With a mixed genre of historical narrative, prophecy, and apocalyptic, the book of Daniel is challenging. As in the book of Revelation, the big picture is clear but the details are often difficult to interpret. The central theme of Daniel is that God is in control, he is at work to safeguard his people, and God's kingdom will one day crush the kingdoms of the world. Similar to other prophetic books, Daniel emphasizes both judgment and hope. Connected with the restoration promises is the hope of resurrection, and Daniel 12:1-3 contains the most explicit Old Testament teaching on this doctrine:

> At that time Michael, the great prince who protects your people, will arise. There will be a time of distress such as has not happened from the beginning of nations until then. But at that time your people—everyone whose name is found written in the book—will be delivered. Multitudes who sleep in the dust of the earth will awake: some to everlasting life, others to shame and everlasting contempt. Those who are wise will shine like the brightness of the heavens, and those who lead many to righteousness, like the stars for ever and ever.

In light of our purposes in this book, Daniel's resurrection prophecy is significant for a number of reasons.

Daniel's prophecy is the first place in Scripture that predicts the resurrection of both the redeemed and the unredeemed. While both groups will be resurrected, the eternal fate of these two groups is different. God's people will awake "to everlasting life" and God's enemies will awake "to shame and everlasting contempt" (Dan 12:2). Since only the redeemed—or those whose names are written in the book—will be delivered and rise to everlasting life, redemptive resurrection is again tied to a right relationship with God.

In his prophecy, Daniel also brings clarity to the nature of the future resurrection. In the most explicit language to this point, Daniel predicts a bodily resurrection for God's people. The hope for God's people is not a disembodied or immaterial experience but rather a future bodily resurrection. Additionally, the promise that those who are raised to everlasting life "will shine like the brightness of the heavens" and "like the stars for ever and ever" (Dan 12:3) hints at a glorified state that will be experienced only in God's presence.

Finally, this resurrection prophecy is closely linked with Daniel's other restoration prophecies, including the coming of the heavenly son of man who will usher in God's last-days kingdom (Dan 7:9-14). Thus, Daniel ties together the eschatological hopes of future resurrection with the coming of the kingdom. Bodily resurrection from the dead is not peripheral for salvation but is rather an essential part of God's plan of redemption. Putting all of this together, we see that Daniel's prophecy of resurrection hope is tethered to a right relationship with God, God's life-giving presence, and the eschatological kingdom of God.

Consistent with the central theme of Daniel, the passage serves as encouragement for God's people who experience persecution. Although there always has been and always will be persecution and suffering in this life, God promises that he will bring justice to the world and reward the godly and punish the ungodly. The great eschatological reversal of resurrection to "everlasting life" for the godly and "everlasting contempt" for the ungodly provides hope in the midst of suffering and persecution. To quote N. T. Wright again, "Death is the last weapon of the tyrant, and the point of the resurrection, despite much misunderstanding, is that death has been defeated."[20] The book of Daniel emphasizes that God is in control and he is at work to safeguard his people, but God's ultimate protection of his people does not come in this

---

[20] N. T. Wright, *Surprised by Hope: Rethinking Heaven, the Resurrection, and the Mission of the Church* (New York: HarperOne, 2008), 50.

life but in the life to come. We would do well to remember this. Even though we often become enamored with the comforts and securities of this life, there are always stark reminders (such as a serious illness, persecution, or the death of a loved one) that our ultimate hope is not and cannot be in this life, but is rather in the everlasting resurrection life to come.

CONCLUSION AND APPLICATION

The prophetic books continue the trajectory that God established at creation and unfolds in redemption. The prophets write about resurrection and tie these hopes to God's relationship with his people, life in God's presence, and the eschatological kingdom of God. That we find more explicit Old Testament resurrection promises in the prophetic books can be attributed to the prophets looking forward to a future restoration, a time when God's favor and blessings would be greater than the old-covenant experience. This restoration experience will be realized in an end-time kingdom, God's presence in the new creation, a renewed relationship with God in the new covenant, and resurrection life.

Table 5.1. Old and new covenants

OLD COVENANT EXPERIENCE	NEW COVENANT RESTORATION
Old covenant (broken by Israel)	New covenant (restored relationship with God)
Physical temple in Jerusalem	New and glorified eschatological temple
Kingdom of Israel under David and his descendants	Eschatological kingdom of God
Life in the land of promise	Resurrection life in the new creation

The hope of the prophetic books is the hope for Christians today. Although we live on this side of Jesus' first coming (in contrast to the Old Testament prophets) and can rejoice in what Christ has already accomplished, we still look forward to the consummation of God's redemptive plan. This life is filled with many blessings, but like God's people in the old covenant, we continue to experience trials, tribulations, persecution, and death. The prophetic books give us hope that God will bring his great eschatological reversal when his last-days kingdom is consummated with Jesus' second coming. God's enemies, including sin and death, will be defeated, and God's people will be resurrected to reign with him in the new creation.

Table 5.2. Unfolding of resurrection in the Old Testament

Genesis 3:15	Implicit promise of resurrection
Psalm 49:7-15	Redemption from death for God's people
Isaiah 25:7-8	God will swallow up death forever and remove the disgrace of his people
Isaiah 26:19	Physical resurrection for God's people
Daniel 12:1-3	Bodily resurrection of redeemed to everlasting life and glory; bodily resurrection of unredeemed to shame and everlasting contempt

Although it is often muted, the biblical foundation for resurrection is present in the Old Testament. To return to Warfield's illustration of the Trinity, the Old Testament teaching on resurrection also "may be likened to a chamber richly furnished but dimly lighted."[21] One of the hallmarks of biblical theology is the progressive revelation of God's redemptive plan, which unfolds throughout the Old Testament. In Genesis 3:15 God's promise that the offspring of the woman will crush the head of the serpent represents an implicit promise of resurrection. In Psalm 49:7-15 the psalmist is convinced that God will redeem his people from death and take them to himself. Isaiah prophesies that God will swallow up death forever (Is 25:7-8) and that there will be a bodily resurrection for God's people (Is 26:19). All of this reaches its Old Testament climax with Daniel's prophecy of physical resurrection for both the redeemed and the unredeemed, one to everlasting life and the other to shame and everlasting contempt (Dan 12:1-3). The Old Testament teaching on resurrection sets the stage for God's revelation in the New Testament, when the lights are turned on.

---

[21]B. B. Warfield, "The Biblical Doctrine of the Trinity," in *The Works of Benjamin B. Warfield*, vol. 2, *Biblical Doctrines* (Grand Rapids, MI: Baker Books, 2000), 141.

Chapter Six

JESUS' LIFE, MINISTRY, AND DEATH ON THE CROSS

Hail the Heav'n-born Prince of Peace!
Hail the Sun of Righteousness!
Light and life to all he brings,
Ris'n with healing in his wings.

Mild he lays his glory by,
Born that man no more may die,
Born to raise the sons of earth,
Born to give them second birth.

CHARLES WESLEY

ONE OF MY FAVORITE PLACES IN THE WORLD is the Highlands of Scotland. Although I have been a number of times, I was actually enamored with the Highlands for years before I was able to visit. Pictures, movies set in the Highlands, and stories from friends captured its beauty, stirring my longing to see and experience the Highlands for myself. When I finally visited, I witnessed the beauty and grandeur I had only glimpsed through pictures, movies, and stories. I hiked in the glens and climbed to the tops of hills and mountains. The pictures, movies, and stories were wonderful, but they were nothing in comparison to experiencing the Highlands of Scotland in person.

In many ways, this is like comparing the old covenant and the new covenant. In the first chapter, I noted that it is common in biblical theology to divide the basic story of redemptive history into creation, fall, and redemption. These three categories correspond to the themes of life, death, and resurrection. The biblical accounts of creation and the fall are short, but the drama of redemption is a long story full of twists and turns, ups and downs. To be sure, salvation in the old covenant is genuine, but it is always forward-looking. Similar to pictures, movies, and stories of the Highlands, the old covenant represents God's promises, prophecies, and pictures of salvation. These were wonderful, but they did not represent the fullness or the reality.

Table 6.1. Contrast between old and new covenant

OLD COVENANT	NEW COVENANT
Promise	Realization/fulfillment
Prophecy	Fulfillment
Picture/type	Reality/antitype

The new covenant represents the realization of God's promises, the fulfillment of prophecies, and the reality of salvation. While the Old Testament records God's promise that the offspring of the woman will crush the head of the serpent, the New Testament reveals the fulfillment of this redemptive plan—that Jesus, as the great and final son of David, will crush the head of the serpent, bringing victory and salvation to God's people. This salvation entails a restored relationship with God, a return to God's life-giving presence, the last-days kingdom ushered in by the Messiah, and victory over death.

In redemptive history, what is surprising is that the new covenant and the eschatological kingdom of God represent a long process and period of time. In describing this reality, Jesus proclaims, "The kingdom of heaven is like a mustard seed, which a man took and planted in his field. Though it is the smallest of all seeds, yet when it grows, it is the largest of garden plants and becomes a tree, so that the birds come and perch in its branches" (Mt 13:31-32). Jesus' words would have perhaps shocked his disciples and hearers. Rather than coming immediately, the kingdom of God will start small and eventually grow into a large and even worldwide kingdom. As the New Testament reveals, the fulfillment of God's eschatological plan will not happen with one coming of the Messiah, but with two comings, and with an unknown but lengthy period of time between those two advents. With the first coming of the Messiah, the last days have begun (Heb 1:1-3; Acts 2:17). God's promises and prophecies of a restored relationship with God, a return to God's presence, the eschatological kingdom of God, and resurrection begin to unfold with the first coming of Jesus Christ, but they will not be consummated until Jesus' second coming. God's program of redemption continues to be drawn out, yet it progresses toward its goal.

In this chapter and the next, I will discuss how the first coming of Jesus continues the unfolding drama of God's plan of redemption. The first coming of Jesus Christ is represented by his life, death, and resurrection, culminating in his ascension into heaven. In this chapter, I will discuss how Jesus' life and death are intimately connected with God's plan of redemption and resurrection hopes. I will reserve my discussion of Jesus' resurrection for the following chapter since an entire chapter devoted to Jesus' resurrection is certainly appropriate in light of the topic of this book.

JESUS AS THE ONE WHO BRINGS RESTORATION WITH GOD

The New Testament writers make it clear that Jesus is the only means by which humanity can be reconciled to God. In 2 Corinthians 5:18 Paul writes, "All this is from God, who reconciled us to himself through Christ." In addition to the many explicit statements like this, the New Testament writers describe Jesus as the second Adam and true Israel. In Romans 5:12-21 and 1 Corinthians 15:42-49, Paul explicitly contrasts Adam and Jesus. Whereas Adam failed and brought sin, condemnation, and death to humanity, Jesus succeeds and brings righteousness, justification, and resurrection life for those united to him.

Although Jesus' identity as true Israel is implicit throughout the New Testament,[1] it is explicit when Jesus declares, "I am the true vine" (Jn 15:1).

---

[1] See, e.g., how the Gospel of Matthew emphasizes that Jesus rehearses the story of Israel through the genealogy, Jesus' escape to and exodus from Egypt, Jesus' testing in the wilderness for forty days, Jesus' new-covenant teaching on a mountain, and Jesus' appointment of twelve disciples.

We often miss the significance of this statement because we are so far removed from the biblical worldview and context. The background for Jesus' statement is the Old Testament description of Israel as God's vineyard or vine (see, e.g., Is 5:1-7; Jer 2:21; Ps 80). In this light, Jesus' statement is remarkable and paradigm shifting. Jesus is the true vine—true Israel. The implications are profound: anyone who desires to be a part of God's new-covenant people must be united to Jesus as the true vine (Jn 15:1-17). As true Israel, Jesus inaugurates his eschatological kingdom and new-covenant people by choosing twelve disciples, echoing the twelve tribes of Israel. God's people will no longer be defined by ethnicity or physical descent from Abraham (Lk 3:7-9; Rom 11:1-24), but rather by their relationship with the one who represents true Israel (Jn 15:1-17; Gal 3:26-29).

As we have seen, Scripture emphasizes that a right relationship with God is the basis for life. Because Jesus is the second Adam and true Israel, he is the only means by which humanity can be reconciled to God. The implication is that a relationship with God through Jesus leads to life. In John 14:6 Jesus proclaims, "I am the way and the truth and the life. No one comes to the Father except through me." Not only does Jesus clarify that a relationship with God the Father comes only through him; he also emphasizes that he is life. Life is found in and through him. Jesus brings these two themes together by proclaiming that a relationship with God and life are found only in him.

JESUS AS THE TEMPLE AND GOD'S PRESENCE

One of the striking things about Jesus' ministry was his teaching and actions related to the temple. On the one hand, Jesus exhibits great respect for the temple and its purity. At the young age of twelve, he remains at the temple as the rest of his family returns home. In response to his parents' anxiety and astonishment upon finding him, Jesus remarks, "Didn't you know I had to be in my Father's house?" (Lk 2:49). When Jesus clears the temple of the moneychangers, he chastises them and proclaims, "Get these out of here! Stop turning my Father's house into a market!" (Jn 2:16). As the disciples reflect on this incident, they are reminded of Psalm 69:9, which reads, "Zeal for your house consumes me." Similarly, in perhaps a later temple cleansing,

Jesus says, "Is it not written: 'My house will be called a house of prayer for all nations'? But you have made it 'a den of robbers'" (Mk 11:17).

Although Jesus exhibits respect and zeal for the temple, he also speaks in judgment of the temple. In the Olivet discourse, Jesus prophesies about the temple's destruction (Mt 24:2; Mk 13:2; Lk 21:6). In the Gospel of Mark, Jesus' cleansing of the temple is sandwiched between the account of his cursing of the fig tree and the disciples' discovery of the fig tree's barrenness (Mk 11:12-25), and Mark is likely inviting us to read these two events together.[2] Just as the fig tree does not bear fruit, the temple is spiritually barren and does not bear fruit.

Jesus' actions and teachings are not limited to the physical temple. On a number of occasions, Jesus refers to himself as the true or greater temple. When the Jews demand to know why Jesus has authority to cleanse the temple, he responds, "Destroy this temple, and I will raise it again in three days" (Jn 2:19). While the Jews are perplexed and indignant at his claim, John clarifies Jesus' intent when he writes, "But the temple he had spoken of was his body" (Jn 2:21). Moreover, Jesus' promise that he would raise the temple in three days was a clear reference to his resurrection. This is confirmed when the disciples recall this incident and believe his words after he was raised from the dead (Jn 2:22). Additionally, in a conflict with the Pharisees about what is lawful to do on the Sabbath, Jesus proclaims, "I tell you that something greater than the temple is here" (Mt 12:6). Jesus is greater than the temple because he is a fuller and more complete realization of God's presence on the earth.

The evidence for Jesus as the presence of God is not limited to his explicit teaching and actions. In fulfillment of Isaiah 7:14, Jesus is called Immanuel, which means "God with us" (Mt 1:22-23). The prologue to the Gospel of John (1:1-18) reveals that Jesus represents God's presence. Jesus, as the eternal Word of God, is referred to as God (Jn 1:1). When the eternal and divine Word of God becomes flesh and dwells with humanity (Jn 1:14), he represents the true temple and God's presence on the earth. A few verses later, John emphasizes that although no one has ever seen God, Jesus as the Son of God has

---

[2]See Mark L. Strauss, *Four Portraits, One Jesus: A Survey of Jesus and the Gospels*, 2nd ed. (Grand Rapids, MI: Zondervan Academic, 2020), 217-18.

made him known (Jn 1:18). Jesus is the perfect and true Son of God who reveals the Father. Although the persons of the Trinity are distinct, to see Jesus is to see the true revelation of God. Finally, Jesus unequivocally proclaims that he is the link between heaven and earth when he tells Nathanael, "Very truly I tell you, you will see 'heaven open, and the angels of God ascending and descending on' the Son of Man" (Jn 1:51). In his first coming, Jesus represents God's presence on the earth, and he is the only link between humanity and God's presence.

Throughout this book, we have seen that life is intimately associated with God's presence. This is true in creation, is confirmed at the fall when Adam and Eve are cast out of God's presence, and is evident in the drama of redemption. The fact that God has chosen to dwell with humanity in the person of his Son implies that redemption and resurrection life will be linked with him. Jesus, as the true temple and the locus of God's presence, is the means by which his people will receive life.

JESUS AS THE MESSIAH AND SON OF GOD

In addition to being the true temple and the mediator between God and humanity, Jesus is the Messiah. Both Jesus' own words and the New Testament writers attest to this fact.[3] According to the Old Testament and Jewish theology, the Messiah is the great and final son of David who ushers in God's last-days kingdom and delivers God's people from their enemies. While the old age was a time of sin, exile, defeat, and persecution, the new age (or messianic age) represents a time of righteousness, restoration, victory, and reigning for God's people. As the great and final son of David, Jesus ushers in and establishes the eschatological kingdom of God, bringing God's kingship to bear on the earth. For our purposes, it is important to recognize two things: Jesus, as the Messiah, reigns over the kingdom of God and all of creation; and Jesus, as the Messiah, rescues God's people, brings them victory, and enables them to be a part of the eschatological kingdom.

As we have seen, there is a close connection in Scripture between reigning with God and life, and it is not inappropriate to understand reigning with

---

[3]See, e.g., Mk 1:1, 15; 8:27-30; Lk 4:14-21; 24:44-49; Jn 4:25-26; Acts 2:36; Rom 1:1-4.

God as humanity's purpose in life. This connection, established in creation, continues throughout redemptive history. The Old Testament prophets often wrote about the eschatological kingdom of God and resurrection life in their restoration prophecies. As we will see, there is also a close connection between Jesus' resurrection and his messianic reign, and between believers' resurrection life and their reign with God. The significance of this should not be missed: the coming of Jesus the Messiah means the inauguration of the kingdom age and the resurrection age.

LIFE AND RESURRECTION IN JESUS

As I sang the hymn "Hark! The Herald Angels Sing" this past Christmas season, I was struck by how the lyrics explicitly connect the first coming of Jesus with his purpose to bring new birth, new creation, and resurrection life. When we sing the words quoted at the beginning of this chapter, we are reminded of Jesus' purpose to conquer death and bring resurrection life. Not only does Jesus represent God's presence, restore humanity's relationship with God, and inaugurate the last-days kingdom; he is the source of life and resurrection.

John begins his Gospel by taking us back to creation. The very first words, "In the beginning," are a clear allusion to Genesis 1:1. The repeated references to Jesus as the "Word" of God and the claim that nothing was made without him (Jn 1:1-3) further emphasize this creation motif. John wants his readers to understand that the coming of Jesus entails a new creation. And so we read, "In him was life, and that life was the light of all mankind" (Jn 1:4). Not only are we taken back to creation; we also see that new-creation life is in Jesus. Just as God gave life in creation through his word, he gives life in new creation through the incarnate Word.

John's statement that life is in Jesus sets the stage for Jesus' mission to bring life to his people through his own life, death, and resurrection. As John continues his theme of new creation, he emphasizes that faith in Jesus leads to being "born of God" and becoming children of God (Jn 1:12-13). In the context of John's Gospel, to be born of God is to be "born again"[4] (Jn 3:3) and

---

[4] Or "born from above"; see the NIV text note for Jn 3:3.

to be "born of the Spirit" (3:5-8). Thus, believers receive spiritual (i.e., of the Holy Spirit) rebirth and new spiritual life. This highlights once again the close relationship between new spiritual life and resurrection life.

In John 5 the emphasis on resurrection is even more explicit. Jesus insists that God the Father raises the dead and gives life (Jn 5:21) and that the Father "has life in himself" (Jn 5:26). But this life-giving prerogative is not limited to the Father; the Son also has authority to give life to others (Jn 5:21) and has been granted by the Father also "to have life in himself" (Jn 5:26). The life that is in Jesus and that Jesus has authority to give is nothing less than both new spiritual life in the present and resurrection life in the future.

The connection between new spiritual life and resurrection life is established in John 5:24-29. Jesus proclaims, "Very truly I tell you, whoever hears my word and believes him who sent me has eternal life and will not be judged but has crossed over from death to life. Very truly I tell you, a time is coming and has now come when the dead will hear the voice of the Son of God and those who hear will live" (Jn 5:24-25). For those who believe in Jesus, eternal life has already begun. Indeed, there is no condemnation for them because they have already crossed over from death to life (Jn 5:24). Moreover, the time has already come when the dead hear the voice of Jesus and "live" (Jn 5:25). To be united to Christ is to be united to God's life-giving presence, to the only mediator between God and humanity, and to the source of life, even life eternal.

Yet Jesus also speaks of a time "when all who are in their graves will hear his voice and come out—those who have done what is good will rise to live, and those who have done what is evil will rise to be condemned" (Jn 5:28-29). Here Jesus speaks of future resurrection—both for God's people and for God's enemies. Believers will rise to bodily resurrection and eternal life, while God's enemies will rise to condemnation. Thus, in John 5:24-29 Jesus makes the connection between new spiritual life and future bodily resurrection explicit: those who receive new spiritual life will inherit resurrection life.

The New Testament reveals many purposes for Jesus' first coming, but perhaps they could all be subsumed under Jesus' purpose to bring life. Jesus makes this purpose explicit when he proclaims, "I have come that they may have life, and have it to the full" (Jn 10:10). God's promise to bring victory and redemption to humanity will be accomplished through Jesus, and his first coming entails the onset of resurrection life and the age of resurrection. Comparing the two ages of redemptive history, Richard Gaffin writes, "This age is the pre-eschatological order, marked by sin, corruption, and death; the age to come is the eschaton of righteousness and life."[5] With the first coming of Jesus, the age to come, the age characterized by life and righteousness, has broken into the old age. Although believers still experience suffering, difficulty, and even death, the great anchor for believers is that eternal life has already begun, that resurrection life has been inaugurated through new spiritual life in Christ, and that this new spiritual life will be consummated through future bodily resurrection.

Table 6.2. Redemptive themes fulfilled in Jesus Christ

OLD TESTAMENT THEME	NEW TESTAMENT FULFILLMENT
Restored relationship with God	Jesus as second Adam and true Israel; Jesus as mediator between God and humanity
God's life-giving presence • Temple as God's presence • Land of promise as a place of life	Jesus • Jesus as the temple • Jesus and access to God's presence
Reigning with God / promise of Messiah	Jesus as the Messiah who ushers in the eschatological kingdom
Life and resurrection	Eternal resurrection life in Jesus

JESUS' RESURRECTION MIRACLES

My favorite part of going to the movies is the previews. Even though I am interested in the movie I am about to watch, the previews almost always spark my interest in two or three future movies I would like to see, often even more than the one I am about to view! Jesus' miracles in his earthly life can be understood as "previews" of what is to come. In Psalm 103:3, David celebrates that God "heals all your diseases," but believers do not experience the fullness of this promise or reality in this life. Jesus' miracles of healing serve as previews and foretastes of the wonderful inheritance to come, that God will one

---

[5]Richard B. Gaffin Jr., *By Faith, Not by Sight: Paul and the Order of Salvation*, 2nd ed. (Phillipsburg, NJ: P&R, 2013), 31.

day, in fulfillment of Psalm 103:3, heal all the diseases of his people. Jesus' casting out demons emphasizes that all God's enemies will be defeated in the new creation. His calming of the storm hints that the cosmic rebellion of creation will be quelled in the new creation.

In addition to healing, casting out demons, and calming the storm, Jesus raises the only son of a widow (Lk 7:11-17); the daughter of Jairus, the synagogue leader (Lk 8:49-56); and his good friend Lazarus from the dead (Jn 11:1-44). These miracles demonstrate Jesus' compassion and his purpose to bring life to his people. Moreover, Jesus' actions demonstrate his authority to give life and raise the dead, something that he has already affirmed in his words (Jn 5:21, 26). But although the son of the widow, the daughter of Jairus, and Lazarus were raised from the dead, they later died. These miracles did not represent the consummation of salvation, just as Jesus' healing of diseases, casting out of demons, and calming of the storm did not represent their final fulfillment. Jesus' miracles of raising people from the dead serve as previews of what is to come. They are signs and foretastes of a greater salvation when God's people will be raised from the dead for eternity.[6]

In light of my purpose in this book, the Lazarus story deserves further discussion. When Jesus hears about Lazarus's sickness, he decides to stay where he is, yet he is confident that "this sickness will not end in death" (Jn 11:4). Jesus says that Lazarus's sickness (and impending death) is "for God's glory so that God's Son may be glorified through it" (Jn 11:4). After his disciples are confused about the state of Lazarus, Jesus tells them plainly, "Lazarus is dead, and for your sake I am glad I was not there, so that you may believe" (Jn 11:14-15).[7] The significance of Jesus' upcoming miracle should not be missed: his raising of Lazarus brings glory to God and the Son. Victory over death is God-glorifying. Although death is the result of sin and is the

---

[6]In addition to Jesus' miracles, Peter raises Tabitha from the dead (Acts 9:36-42), and Paul raises Eutychus from the dead (Acts 20:7-12). These miracles, in addition to the Old Testament resurrection miracles I previously highlighted, also serve as previews of future resurrection.

[7]From this interaction with his disciples, Jesus reveals two important things about his motivation in ministry: he does all things (1) for the glory of God (Jn 11:4) and (2) for the edification of his disciples' faith (Jn 11:15). Jesus' motivation serves as an example of what our own ministry motivation should be—that we do all things for the glory of God and for the edification of others. I am grateful to Allen Mawhinney, who pointed this out in my Gospels class at Reformed Theological Seminary, Orlando, Spring 2002.

great enemy of God and humanity, God is the giver of life, and Jesus came to bring life—abundant life, eternal life, resurrection life. In this way, the Lazarus story provides a powerful reminder of Jesus' purpose.

The central theme of the Lazarus story comes into focus when Jesus proclaims, "I am the resurrection and the life. The one who believes in me will live, even though they die; and whoever lives by believing in me will never die" (Jn 11:25-26). Similar to other passages in John's Gospel, Jesus' miracles and words go hand in hand. As he is about to raise Lazarus from the dead, Jesus affirms in his teaching that he has power over death and that he is the key to life and resurrection. In the context of the Gospel, Jesus' words point to four realities: (1) Jesus intimates that he is about to raise Lazarus from the dead; (2) Jesus points forward to his own resurrection from the dead; (3) Jesus implies that resurrection life begins when people believe in him;[8] (4) Jesus promises that those who believe in him will receive bodily resurrection in the future.[9] Thus, Jesus' miracle of raising Lazarus from the dead highlights his power over death, foreshadows his own resurrection, and demonstrates that he gives life to all who believe in him. Within the Gospel of John, Jesus' miracles are meant to provoke faith. The story of Lazarus encourages us to have faith in the one who holds power over death and holds the power of resurrection life.

JESUS' PREDICTIONS OF HIS DEATH
AND RESURRECTION

The four Gospels include numerous examples of Jesus' predictions of his death and resurrection, and I offer only a small sample here to emphasize that his death and resurrection are essential to God's redemptive plan. In the Gospel of Mark, after Peter confesses that Jesus is the Messiah (Mk 8:29), Jesus begins to define his messiahship and predicts his death and resurrection in three conversations with his disciples (Mk 8:31-38; 9:30-37; 10:32-45).[10] In these conversations, Jesus clarifies his messianic purposes, emphasizes the necessity of his death and resurrection, and calls his disciples to service and

---

[8]See again Jn 5:24-25.
[9]See again Jn 5:28-29.
[10]See also the discussion in Strauss, *Four Portraits*, 228-48.

sacrifice. The capstone to Jesus' teaching in these conversations is in Mark 10:45 when Jesus says, "For even the Son of Man did not come to be served, but to serve, and to give his life as a ransom for many." On the one hand, Jesus states that he will serve by giving his life as a ransom for others. On the other hand, Jesus' words are an implicit call to service and sacrifice for his disciples and all who would follow Jesus. To follow Jesus is to be called to a life of service and sacrifice.

These words and their implications were no doubt shocking to Jesus' disciples and represent a complete reorientation of their understanding of the messianic kingdom. Jesus, the Messiah, came to serve and to give his life for others. If the disciples want to follow Jesus the Messiah, they must answer the call to service and sacrifice. Moreover, Jesus' conversations with his disciples and his predictions emphasize this all-important truth: Jesus is cognizant of his future death and resurrection and is laser-focused on that goal. The reason for this is that his death and resurrection are intimately connected with God's plan of redemption and his purpose to provide resurrection life.

THE DEATH OF JESUS

The life and teaching of Jesus are of utmost importance for the Christian faith, but they are void of their meaning without Jesus' death and resurrection. As the New Testament makes clear, the death of Jesus is essential to God's plan of redemption and closely associated with the themes we have traced. In regard to a relationship with God, Paul writes that believers have been reconciled to God through Jesus' death (Rom 5:10) and that "God presented Christ as a sacrifice of atonement" (Rom 3:25) so that we can be justified (i.e., forgiven of sin and declared righteous; Rom 3:21-26). Not only are believers reconciled to God through Christ's death; they have received access to God's presence through the blood of Jesus (Heb 10:19-22). Additionally, we learn from Colossians 1 that Christ's death is not only the means of reconciliation with God (Col 1:21-22); it is also the means by which God has rescued believers from the dominion of darkness and brought them into the kingdom of Christ (Col 1:13-14). While all these themes could receive a chapter- or book-length treatment, my purpose in this section is to discuss how Christ's death represents a sacrifice for life. Christ gave himself as a sacrifice so that others could receive life.

Because death is the consequence of sin, there must be a sacrifice in order for God to bring resurrection life to his people. This has been true throughout the history of redemption. In Genesis 3:21 the Lord makes garments of skin for Adam and Eve and clothes them, communicating that only God can cover the sin and shame of humanity. The provision of garments of skin required the killing of an animal, and this animal becomes a substitutionary sacrifice so that Adam and Eve can have life. After the Lord prevents Abraham from sacrificing Isaac, he provides a ram for Abraham to sacrifice as a burnt offering instead of his son Isaac (Gen 22:13-14). The blood of the Passover lamb is the substitute for the firstborn in Israel when the Lord takes the life of all the firstborn in Egypt (Ex 12:1-30). Finally, the Lord institutes the sacrificial system in the book of Leviticus, and these sacrifices, culminating in the Day of Atonement (Lev 16:1-34), provide atonement for sins and serve as substitutionary sacrifices so that God's people can live in his presence.

As Scripture unfolds, it becomes clear that the animal sacrifices of the old covenant were merely pictures or types. Indeed, the author of Hebrews clarifies that animal sacrifices can never take away sins (Heb 10:4). In the history of redemption, they were significant because they pointed to a greater reality. God accepted the old-covenant sacrifices because he knew that a greater sacrifice (i.e., the reality or antitype) was to come in the future.[11] The Old Testament prophesied about this greater sacrifice, a "suffering servant" who would be pierced for transgressions, crushed for iniquities, punished for the sin of God's people, and made an offering for sin (Is 52:13–53:12). As the one who is punished by God and the sacrifice for sin, he is also the one who "will see his offspring" (Is 53:10) and "will justify many" (Is 53:11). The sacrifice of the servant is for a specific purpose—to bring life to others.

The New Testament communicates that Jesus is the fulfillment of the Old Testament sacrifices and the prophecy of the suffering servant. Jesus' death

---

[11]This is an implication of Rom 3:25, where Paul writes that God "presented Christ as a sacrifice of atonement . . . to demonstrate his righteousness, because in his forbearance he had left the sins committed beforehand unpunished."

on the cross serves as the final and ultimate sacrifice to bring life to God's people. Jesus is "the Lamb of God, who takes away the sin of the world" (Jn 1:29). "God presented Christ as a sacrifice of atonement, through the shedding of his blood" (Rom 3:25). In his death, Jesus is forsaken by God (Ps 22:1; Mk 15:34), punished by God (Is 53:4), stricken by God (Is 53:4), and crushed by God (Is 53:10). Peter alludes to the song of the suffering servant and emphasizes that Christ "suffered for you" and "bore our sins" (1 Pet 2:21-25), yet this was not without purpose. Jesus' death was not an accidental or haphazard event but was a divinely orchestrated event that is essential to God's plan of redemption.

In another allusion to the song of the suffering servant, Jesus says that he "did not come to be served, but to serve, and to give his life as a ransom for many" (Mk 10:45). Here we should reflect on an astounding reality. The Son of God, God incarnate, and the king of creation did not come to be served but to serve. Moreover, Jesus emphasizes here that he came to serve in a specific way—to give his life as a ransom. By serving as the ransom, Jesus gives life to his people. Jesus' life-giving purpose is seen in the irony of the crucifixion account. As Jesus is on the cross, some of the witnesses mock him by saying, "Come down from the cross and save yourself!" (Mk 15:30). The chief priests and teachers of the law mock him, saying, "He saved others . . . but he can't save himself!" (Mk 15:31). The irony is that Jesus' purpose is not to save himself. By remaining on the cross and enduring the pain and scorn of death, he brings life to others.[12]

Many other passages connect Jesus' death with God's life-giving purposes. In 1 Corinthians 1:18 Paul says that the message of the cross is foolishness to those who are perishing but it is the power of God to those who are being saved. In this context, believers are saved specifically from sin and death (perishing), implying that they are saved for life. Peter emphasizes that Christ

---

[12]In the gospel accounts, the Roman centurion senses on some level the significance of Jesus at his crucifixion. In Mk 15:39 the centurion proclaims, "Surely this man was the Son of God!" (cf. Mt 27:54), while in Lk 23:47 he proclaims, "Surely this was a righteous man." Significantly, one statement alludes to Jesus as Messiah (Son of God), and the other to Jesus' righteousness, two realities that serve as the basis for Jesus' resurrection to life after death. The resurrection vindicates Jesus and demonstrates that his crucifixion and death were unjust and that he is indeed the Messiah and righteous.

bore our sins on the cross "so that we might die to sins and *live* for right-eousness" (1 Pet 2:24, emphasis added). While the fall resulted in sin and death for Adam and all of humanity, the cross restores us to life and right-eousness. Similarly, Paul writes, "And he died for all, that those who live should no longer live for themselves but for him who died for them and was raised again" (2 Cor 5:15). When Jesus takes the punishment of his people on himself, his purpose is to bring life to them.

The crucifixion of Jesus is an eschatological event of utmost significance, and the events accompanying the crucifixion attest to this. Before his death, darkness covered the land (Mt 27:45). The moment Jesus gave up his spirit, the temple curtain was torn and an earthquake occurred (Mt 27:51-52). The rending of the temple curtain from top to bottom emphasizes that this was a work of God and that access to God has been accomplished through Jesus' death. Jesus' sacrifice provides forgiveness of sins, reconciles humanity to God, and allows God's people to have unhindered access to him. Although the enigmatic reference to the resurrection of many holy people (Mt 27:52-53) should most likely be connected with Jesus' resurrection (since Matthew emphasizes that these holy people "came out of the tombs *after* Jesus' resur-rection" [Mt 27:53, emphasis added]), Matthew's inclusion of the event at Jesus' crucifixion highlights the importance of Jesus' death for God's resur-rection and life-giving purposes.

The significance of Jesus' death cannot be overstated.[13] In 1 Corinthians, Paul emphasizes that he preaches "Christ crucified" (1 Cor 1:23) and that he "resolved to know nothing while [he] was with [the Corinthians] except Jesus Christ and him crucified" (1 Cor 2:2). The Old Testament "pictures," the prophecy of the suffering servant in Isaiah, and the New Testament evidence make it clear: Christ's death is essential in God's plan of redemption. In John 12:24, when speaking about his impending death, Jesus says, "Very truly I tell you, unless a kernel of wheat falls to the ground and dies, it remains only a single seed. But if it dies, it produces many seeds" (Jn 12:24). Jesus' death is not meaningless. It is a sacrificial death that brings life to God's

---

[13]For a discussion of the role of Jesus' death in the new-creation storyline, see G. K. Beale, *A New Testament Biblical Theology: The Unfolding of the Old Testament in the New* (Grand Rapids, MI: Baker Academic, 2011), 905-8.

people and reorients their lives around the Lord Jesus. G. K. Beale writes, "The key issue here is that Christ had to give something for the redemption of his people to occur, and what he gave was his life, which is essentially the cost of redemption."[14] Jesus Christ gave his life, the cost of redemption, so that his people can have life. The lyrics from "How Deep the Father's Love for Us" by Stuart Townend capture this glorious exchange: "His dying breath has brought me life."[15] Jesus' dying breath and finished work on the cross have brought life to his people. Jesus has paid the ransom for sin so that believers can live—and that ransom was nothing less than his life for their life.

CONCLUSION AND APPLICATION

With the first coming of Jesus, the age of resurrection has dawned. The New Testament affirms that Jesus represents the presence of God, that Jesus is the only mediator between God and humanity, and that Jesus is the Messiah who ushers in God's last-days kingdom. These themes are intimately connected with life and resurrection. Consequently, it is not surprising that the New Testament also communicates that Jesus is the one who holds power over death and possesses resurrection life. Jesus affirms his power over death through his teaching and his miracles, yet he also teaches that he will be crucified, that he will give his life as a ransom for others, and that he will be raised to life. Jesus' explicit predictions of his death and resurrection emphasize that they are essential for God's plan of redemption.

As the fulfillment of Genesis 3:15, Jesus is the one who crushes the head of the serpent and brings victory to humanity. But for this to happen, Jesus must conquer sin and death. As the Gospels unfold, this happens in a most unexpected way—through Jesus' offering himself as a sacrifice and atonement for sin. We should reflect on the cost of our salvation: nothing less than the sacrificial death of Jesus could accomplish salvation and bring new life in Christ. Without Jesus as the suffering servant, we could not be reconciled to God, could not have access to God's presence, could not be a part of God's kingdom, and could not inherit eternal life—both new spiritual life in the

---

[14]Beale, *New Testament Biblical Theology*, 486.
[15]Stuart Townend, "How Deep the Father's Love for Us," Thankyou Music, 1995, www.stuarttownend .co.uk/song/how-deep-the-fathers-love-for-us/.

present and bodily resurrection life in the future. This should lead us to gratitude and worship, and move us to service. Just as Jesus came to serve, the path for his disciples is one of service and sacrifice (Mk 10:45; Phil 2:1-11). As those who have been reconciled through Christ's death, our call is no longer to live for ourselves but rather to live for Jesus, who died for us and was raised to life (2 Cor 5:15).

In his life and sacrificial death, Jesus has accomplished much. But this is not the end of the story. Sin and death are not defeated only through Christ's life and death. The resurrection of Jesus is essential to God's plan of redemption and his life-giving purposes. And this is the subject of the next chapter.

Chapter Seven

THE RESURRECTION
OF JESUS

It's a beautiful day!

U2

IN THE OPENING TRACK of their album *All That You Can't Leave Behind*, U2 sings, "It's a beautiful day!" In an interview, Bono maintained that the song is a celebration of the beauty and joy that can be experienced even in the midst of great loss and despair.[1] Although not about resurrection, the song is fitting for two reasons. First, the lyrics, the mood, and the tone of the song provide an apt description of how Christians should view Easter and Jesus' resurrection. Second, the resurrection of Jesus is precisely what allows believers to have hope and joy in the midst of loss and despair.

For Christians, there should be no greater and more joyous day than the day of Jesus' resurrection. When comparing the emphasis that the church has given to various days of celebration (e.g., Christmas, Good Friday, Easter), N. T. Wright contends, "Easter . . . should be the center. Take that away and

---

[1]U2, "U2—Beautiful Day (The Making Of)," YouTube video, October 7, 2020, https://www.youtube.com/watch?v=zm-5lK-16_A; "'Beautiful Day' by U2," Songfacts, https://www.songfacts.com/facts/u2/beautiful-day.

there is, almost literally, nothing left."[2] Moreover, Wright emphasizes that Easter calls for a day, or even a season, of celebration. "Is it any wonder people find it hard to believe in the resurrection of Jesus if we don't throw our hats in the air? . . . This is our greatest day. We should put the flags out."[3] The reason Easter should be our greatest day is that the resurrection of Jesus changes every other day, from now and into eternity. For those who are united to Christ, their future is the future of their Savior, and this reality changes everything.

That Easter is not usually viewed or celebrated in this way demonstrates again that Christians all too often possess a theology of Christ's sacrificial death but an underdeveloped theology of Jesus' resurrection. Paul's words in 1 Corinthians 15:17, "If Christ has not been raised, your faith is futile; you are still in your sins," are striking. Without Jesus' resurrection, there is no forgiveness of sins. Sadly, far too many Christians do not understand this connection between Jesus' resurrection and forgiveness of sins. They can readily articulate the importance of Jesus' death for forgiveness (Rom 3:25) but struggle to connect Jesus' resurrection with forgiveness. Paul's statement in 1 Corinthians 15:17 demonstrates that the problem was not with the earliest followers of Jesus or the writers of the New Testament. The problem is with us.

Over and over again, the writers of the New Testament emphasize the importance of Jesus' resurrection. Consider Paul's words in 1 Corinthians 15:1-8:

> Now, brothers and sisters, I want to remind you of the gospel I preached to you, which you received and on which you have taken your stand. By this gospel you are saved, if you hold firmly to the word I preached to you. Otherwise, you have believed in vain.
>
> For what I received I passed on to you as of first importance: that Christ died for our sins according to the Scriptures, that he was buried, that he was raised on the third day according to the Scriptures, and that he appeared to Cephas, and then to the Twelve. After that, he appeared to more than five hundred of the brothers and sisters at the same time, most of whom

---

[2]N. T. Wright, *Surprised by Hope: Rethinking Heaven, the Resurrection, and the Mission of the Church* (New York: HarperOne, 2008), 23.
[3]Wright, *Surprised by Hope*, 256-57.

are still living, though some have fallen asleep. Then he appeared to James, then to all the apostles, and last of all he appeared to me also, as to one abnormally born.

In this passage, Paul spells out the connection between the gospel and Jesus' death and resurrection, and emphasizes that this gospel is of central importance—both for Jesus' mission and the apostolic mission. The larger context of 1 Corinthians 15 and the teaching of the New Testament communicate three significant aspects related to the resurrection of Jesus: his resurrection is a historical event, his resurrection is essential to his identity and mission, and his resurrection is essential for the salvation of God's people.

Regarding the first item, I assume and presuppose the truth of Scripture and the historicity of Jesus' resurrection in this book. The second and third items, however, are highly significant for the purposes of this book. My purpose in this chapter is to discuss the significance of Jesus' resurrection in relation to his identity and mission, and the salvation of God's people. I will focus my discussion on the following topics: (1) the resurrection as vindication of Jesus as the Messiah, (2) the resurrection as vindication of Jesus' righteousness, (3) Jesus as the second Adam, (4) Jesus' resurrection and the new age, and (5) Jesus' resurrection, ascension, and enthronement.

THE RESURRECTION AS VINDICATION OF JESUS AS MESSIAH

The New Testament makes it clear that Jesus is the Messiah, the long-awaited king from the line of David who ushers in God's last-days kingdom. The term *Christ*, which people today often misunderstand as another name for Jesus, is the Greek term for the Hebrew *Messiah*. Although in the Gospels Jesus sometimes commands people to be silent about his identity (most likely so that he can define his messiahship in his timing), there are other times when he explicitly claims to be the Messiah (Mt 16:16-20; Lk 4:16-21; Jn 4:25-26).

The problem for those who encountered Jesus is that he often did not fulfill the typical Jewish expectations of the Messiah, at least in the way they expected. While John the Baptist is convinced of Jesus' identity early in his ministry (Mt 3:11-14; Lk 3:15-18; Jn 1:29-34), John's later imprisonment (and impending death) does not match up with his messianic expectations, and John sends his disciples to inquire whether Jesus really is the Messiah, or whether they should start looking for someone else (Mt 11:1-3). Certainly, for the apostle Peter, suffering, rejection, and the killing of the Messiah were not part of his messianic expectations (Mk 8:31-32). And with Jesus' death on the cross, the disciples had significant doubts about Jesus fulfilling their messianic hopes (Lk 24:17-21).

Since the Old Testament describes the Messiah as a king from the line of David who brings God's last-days kingdom, defeats Israel's enemies, and ushers in an age of unprecedented peace and righteousness, we can understand the disciples' confusion over Jesus' teaching about his death and their dashed hopes when his death came to pass. But this is one reason the resurrection of Jesus is so important. Jesus' resurrection serves as proof that he is indeed the messianic king. Even though it was God's will for him to suffer and serve as the atoning sacrifice for sin, death is not the final word for Jesus. And although the suffering and death of the Messiah were prophesied in the Old Testament, the Old Testament also clarifies that death is not the final outcome for the Messiah (Ps 22; Is 52:13–53:12).[4]

In addition to the Old Testament prophecies, the New Testament communicates that Jesus' resurrection serves as vindication that he is the Messiah. In 1 Timothy 3:16 Paul's proclamation that "he appeared in the flesh, / was vindicated by the Spirit" is a clear reference to Jesus' vindication as a result of his bodily resurrection through the power of the Holy Spirit. Moreover, in his Pentecost sermon Peter proclaims,

> Fellow Israelites, I can tell you confidently that the patriarch David died and was buried, and his tomb is here to this day. But he was a prophet and knew that God had promised him on oath that he would place one of his descendants on his throne. Seeing what was to come, he spoke of the resurrection

---

[4]David Allen notes that the death of Christ was a "problem" for Jesus' earliest followers and says that "the early church needed to find justification or support for what was so 'unexpected' or counter-intuitive," and consequently appealed to the Old Testament Scriptures for this purpose. *According to the Scriptures: The Death of Christ in the Old Testament and the New* (London: SCM Press, 2018), 10-11.

of the Messiah, that he was not abandoned to the realm of the dead, nor did his body see decay. God has raised this Jesus to life, and we are all witnesses of it. (Acts 2:29-32)[5]

Although Jesus was forsaken by God as he took on himself the sin of his people on the cross (Mk 15:34), God did not ultimately abandon Jesus to the grave. Rather, God raised Jesus to life, and Jesus reigns at God's right hand (Acts 2:32-35). Consequently, Peter proclaims, "God has made this Jesus, whom you crucified, both Lord and Messiah" (Acts 2:36). N. T. Wright notes, "Crucifixion meant that the kingdom hadn't come, not that it had. Crucifixion of a would-be Messiah meant that he wasn't the Messiah, not that he was. When Jesus was crucified, every single disciple knew what it meant: we backed the wrong horse. The game is over."[6] The resurrection, therefore, is essential to Jesus' purpose and identity. By raising Jesus from the dead, God declares that Jesus is indeed the Lord and Messiah.

THE RESURRECTION AS VINDICATION OF JESUS' RIGHTEOUSNESS

Not only does the resurrection serve as vindication of Jesus as the Messiah; it also serves as vindication of his righteousness. Once again, Psalm 22 and Isaiah 52:13–53:12 are instructive. The picture of Psalm 22 is that David is a righteous sufferer, one who experiences unjust persecution and tribulation at the hands of his enemies (Ps 22:6-18). As a result of his suffering, David ponders whether God has forsaken him and questions why the Lord has not delivered him (Ps 22:1-5). In a turning point, he cries out to the Lord for help and deliverance (Ps 22:19-21). However, the psalm does not end with David's suffering and unjust treatment; it ends with David's vindication (Ps 22:22-31).

Jesus' cry of Psalm 22:1 at his crucifixion calls attention to the fact that he is forsaken by God as he takes on himself the sin of his people, but the psalm's ending reminds us that God does not ultimately abandon his people,

---

[5]See also Acts 4:10; 13:26-37; 17:31.
[6]Wright, *Surprised by Hope*, 40. On Jesus' resurrection as vindication of his messiahship and sonship, see Murray J. Harris, *From Grave to Glory: Resurrection in the New Testament* (Grand Rapids, MI: Academie Books, 1990), 165-68.

and that God has not ultimately abandoned Jesus.[7] Just as God vindicated David and delivered him from death, so God vindicates Jesus through death because his suffering was unjust and because he was righteous. In this sense, Psalm 22 is typology. David was righteous in that the suffering and persecution he experienced were unjust, but he was by no means perfectly righteous. Jesus, on the other hand, was perfectly righteous and without sin. David is delivered from a premature death, but Jesus is delivered after death through resurrection.[8]

Numerous places in the New Testament testify that Jesus was righteous and without sin. According to Hebrews, Jesus was "tempted in every way, just as we are—yet he did not sin" (Heb 4:15) and was able to offer himself as an "unblemished" sacrifice to God (Heb 9:14).[9] In his Pentecost sermon Peter describes Jesus as "a man accredited by God" (Acts 2:22) who was put to death "with the help of wicked men" (Acts 2:23). The implication is that Jesus was innocent and that those who put him to death were the sinful ones. Similarly, in his synagogue sermon Paul argues that the Israelites "found no proper ground for a death sentence" yet still asked for Jesus to be executed (Acts 13:28). In their respective sermons, Peter and Paul both connect Jesus' innocence with his resurrection by declaring, "But God raised him from the dead" (Acts 2:24; 13:30).

---

[7]See Richard P. Belcher Jr., *The Messiah and the Psalms: Preaching Christ from All the Psalms* (Glasgow: Mentor, 2006), 166-72. Belcher argues that Jesus' use of the first line of Ps 22 invites the reader to interpret the entire psalm in light of Christ's work (166-67). While the first twenty-one verses should be interpreted in light of Christ's death, the subsequent verses should be interpreted in light of Christ's resurrection (171).

[8]Although the New Testament writers do not explicitly cite Ps 22 for Jesus' resurrection, two references to Ps 22 in Hebrews support such an understanding. First, the author of Hebrews quotes Ps 22:22 ("I will declare your name to my brothers and sisters; / in the assembly I will sing your praises" [Heb 2:12]), from the vindication section of the psalm, and applies it to Jesus. The context of this reference in Hebrews is Jesus' resurrected and glorified state in heaven (Heb 2:9). Second, there is a possible allusion to Ps 22:24 when the author writes, "During the days of Jesus' life on earth, he offered up prayers and petitions with fervent cries and tears to the one who could save him from death, and he was *heard* because of his reverent submission" (Heb 5:7, emphasis added). Just as God heard David's prayer and delivered him from death, God also heard Jesus' cry and delivered him after death through resurrection. See also Allen P. Ross, who cites Heb 5:7 as an allusion to Ps 22:24 in *A Commentary on the Psalms*, vol. 1, *1–41*, Kregel Exegetical Library (Grand Rapids, MI: Kregel, 2011), 550.

[9]See also 2 Cor 5:21; 1 Pet 2:22; 1 Jn 3:5.

In his first epistle, Peter explicitly claims that Jesus was righteous and sinless when he writes, "He committed no sin, / and no deceit was found in his mouth" (1 Pet 2:22). Peter's claim here is rather astounding, especially in light of Peter's relationship with Jesus. Peter was a disciple and good friend of Jesus, and he traveled with him on a regular basis. When I travel with other people, I usually find out very quickly that they are sinners, and they find out just as quickly that I am a sinner. Whether from the hassle of packing, the challenges of being on time, the close quarters with others, or the anxiety of a new situation, traveling with friends and family is often stressful. Moreover, Jesus often rebuked Peter for his sin. Again, in my own experience, those who are rebuked for sin often become defensive and accuse the other person. But Peter does none of that. After traveling with Jesus for many years and regularly being rebuked by Jesus, Peter maintains that Jesus was sinless.

Peter's quotation of Isaiah 53:9 is also noteworthy. The song of the suffering servant explicitly describes the righteousness, sinlessness, and innocence of God's servant. But as the song clarifies, suffering and death are not the end of the journey for the servant. The ending is vindication and exaltation. In his willingness to suffer for his people, the servant is silent in the midst of his oppression (Is 53:7) and without sin, violence, or deceit (Is 53:9). For this reason, there is life, vindication, and victory for God's servant after death (Is 53:10-12). Because of his righteousness and innocence, death is not the final word for God's servant. Life, vindication, and victory are the final word.

The song of the suffering servant is fulfilled in the life, death, and resurrection of Jesus. The New Testament writers regularly appeal to and cite the passage as Old Testament evidence for Jesus' sinlessness and sacrificial death.[10] But in addition to serving as a prophecy of Jesus' sinlessness and sacrificial death, the song predicts Jesus' vindication and exaltation after his suffering. As J. Alex Motyer notes, the verbs *raised, lifted up,* and *highly exalted* in Isaiah 52:13 hint at the identity of the suffering servant and are reminiscent of Jesus' resurrection, ascension, and heavenly exaltation.[11] This movement

---

[10]See, e.g., Mt 8:17; 26:63; Mk 14:60-61; 15:4-5; Lk 22:37; Jn 1:29; Acts 8:32-33; 1 Pet 2:21-25.

[11]J. Alex Motyer, *The Prophecy of Isaiah: An Introduction and Commentary* (Downers Grove, IL: IVP Academic, 1993), 424.

from humiliation to exaltation indicates that the song of the suffering servant might have served as the Old Testament background for the Christ hymn in Philippians 2:6-11.[12]

As the second Adam (Rom 5:12-21) and the perfect image of God (Col 1:15; Heb 1:3), Jesus fulfilled and embodied all that God created humanity to be. Whereas Adam failed and earned death, Jesus was perfectly righteous. And although he suffered death, Jesus was vindicated by God and earned resurrection life because he was perfectly righteous. In C. S. Lewis's *The Lion, the Witch and the Wardrobe*, Aslan's description of his death and resurrection provides an apt illustration:

> "It means," said Aslan, "that though the Witch knew the Deep Magic, there is a magic deeper still which she did not know. Her knowledge goes back only to the dawn of time. But if she could have looked a little further back, into the stillness and the darkness before Time dawned, she would have read there a different incantation. She would have known that when a willing victim who had committed no treachery was killed in a traitor's stead, the Table would crack and Death itself would start working backward."[13]

On account of his righteous life and perfect sacrifice, God vindicated Jesus through his resurrection, and Jesus therefore conquered death. Peter proclaims that "it was impossible for death to keep its hold on him" (Acts 2:24). The resurrection of Jesus serves as a vindication of his sinlessness, perfect righteousness, and undeserving death. As Geerhardus Vos notes, "Resurrection had annulled the sentence of condemnation."[14]

Jesus' resurrection is linked not only with his vindication, but also with the vindication of his people. As discussed, this is evident in the song of the suffering servant. Not only is the righteous servant vindicated; he is also the one who justifies many (Is 53:11). The New Testament sheds more light on this relationship. The biblical doctrine of justification should be understood in forensic categories. God is the righteous judge, and as a result of

---

[12]See John N. Oswalt, *The Book of Isaiah: Chapters 40–66*, New International Commentary on the Old Testament (Grand Rapids, MI: Eerdmans, 1998), 378-79, 405-8.

[13]C. S. Lewis, *The Lion, the Witch and the Wardrobe* (New York: HarperTrophy, 1950), 178-79.

[14]Geerhardus Vos, *The Pauline Eschatology* (1930; repr., Phillipsburg, NJ: P&R, 1994), 151. See also Harris, *From Grave to Glory*, 168-69.

sin, humanity stands condemned before God and deserving of his wrath. But the good news is that sinners can be justified and restored to a right relationship with God through faith in Jesus. To be justified is to be forgiven of sin and declared righteous before God. Whereas sinners previously stood condemned before God, believers are now forgiven, declared righteous, and restored to a right relationship with God through faith in Jesus (Rom 3:21-31; Gal 2:15-16).

Justification is a most important biblical doctrine, but many Christians fail to see how the resurrection of Jesus is related to the justification of believers. The key to putting this together comes in Romans 4:25, where Paul writes, "[Jesus] was delivered over to death for our sins and was raised to life for our justification." Because Jesus was vindicated and declared righteous in his resurrection, those who are united to Christ by faith are also vindicated, justified, and declared righteous. For believers to be united to the risen and vindicated Christ is to have him as their representative.[15] In his resurrection, Jesus becomes the basis on which those who are united to Christ can also be vindicated.

This means there is no justification without Christ's resurrection. This is the reason Paul writes, "And if Christ has not been raised, your faith is futile; you are still in your sins" (1 Cor 15:17). Along these lines, Wright notes, "Sin is the root cause of death; if death has been defeated, it must mean that sin has been dealt with. But if the Messiah has not been raised, we are still in a world where sin reigns supreme and undefeated so that the foundational Christian belief, that God has dealt with our sins in Christ, is based on thin air and is reduced to whistling in the dark."[16] Jesus' resurrection means that sin and death have been defeated. Consequently, without the resurrection of Jesus, there is no salvation. The New Testament makes clear that salvation and all the blessings of salvation come through union with Christ. Without Jesus' vindication and resurrection, there is no hope for justification and resurrection for those who

---

[15]For the close connection between resurrection and justification in Paul, see Richard B. Gaffin Jr., *By Faith, Not by Sight: Paul and the Order of Salvation*, 2nd ed. (Phillipsburg, NJ: P&R, 2013), 91-122, and Adrian Warnock, *Raised with Christ: How the Resurrection Changes Everything* (Wheaton, IL: Crossway, 2010), 117-31.

[16]Wright, *Surprised by Hope*, 247.

are united to him. Justification, therefore, is not only the result of Jesus' perfect life and sacrificial death; it is also the result of Jesus' resurrection.[17]

JESUS AS THE SECOND ADAM

Adam, the first representative for humanity, failed to obey God's word and faithfully serve as God's prophet, priest, and king. Adam's sin and failure brought about death for Adam and all humanity. But the coming of Jesus means that a new representative is available for humanity. Just as life was central to the creation account, so also life is central to new creation in Jesus (Jn 1:1-18; 3:13-16). Two passages in Paul demonstrate the contrast between Adam as the first representative for humanity and Christ as the second representative.

In Romans 5:12-21 Paul contrasts Adam's sin and failure with Jesus' righteousness and victory. Paul's train of thought in this passage is important. Whereas Adam's disobedience and sin brought condemnation and death, Jesus' obedience and righteousness brings justification and life. Thus, Adam's sin is contrasted with Jesus' righteousness and obedience, condemnation under Adam is contrasted with justification in Jesus, and death as the result of sin is contrasted with life as the result of Jesus' righteousness, vindication, and resurrection.[18] Jesus' righteousness, vindication, and resurrection life serve as the basis for the righteousness, justification, and life of his people who are united to him by faith. And the result of Christ's work is that justification, righteousness, and life now reign in God's people as opposed to sin, death, and condemnation.

Paul provides a similar contrast in 1 Corinthians 15:21-22 when he writes, "For since death came through a man, the resurrection of the dead comes also through a man. For as in Adam all die, so in Christ all will be made alive." Whereas sin, righteousness, condemnation, justification, death, and life were Paul's focus in Romans 5:12-21, Paul zeroes in on the contrast between life

---

[17]G. K. Beale also emphasizes that Christ's death has received much more attention in theology (in this instance in relation to the doctrine of justification) than Jesus' resurrection; see *A New Testament Biblical Theology: The Unfolding of the Old Testament in the New* (Grand Rapids, MI: Baker Academic, 2011), 492.

[18]See Gaffin, *By Faith*, 55-56; Herman Ridderbos similarly emphasizes that Adam and Jesus represent the entrance to two different worlds, eons, and "creations"; see *Paul: An Outline of His Theology*, trans. John Richard de Witt (Grand Rapids, MI: Eerdmans, 1975), 61.

and death in 1 Corinthians 15 because resurrection is his focus. Those who are united to the first Adam receive what the first Adam earned through sin: death. But those who are united to the last Adam receive what Jesus earned through his righteousness and resurrection: resurrection life.

As the second Adam, Jesus gives life to others. Whereas Adam was merely "a living being," in his resurrection Jesus became "a life-giving spirit" (1 Cor 15:45).[19] Whereas Adam should have provided physical and spiritual life for his offspring, he instead brought sin and death. As the second Adam, Jesus provides eternal resurrection life for his people.[20] Thus, Jesus is "the Inaugurator of the new humanity."[21] Because of his resurrection, Jesus can serve as life-giving spirit and the source of resurrection life for others.[22] Moreover, John 2:19-22 clarifies that Jesus' resurrection represents the rebuilding of the temple, the place of God's presence. As the resurrected and glorified temple and life-giving spirit, Jesus ascends into heaven and pours out the Holy Spirit on his people. On account of union with the risen Christ and the indwelling of the Spirit, believers are the body of Christ (1 Cor 12:27) and the temple (1 Cor 3:16-17; 6:19; Eph 2:19-22). Those who are indwelled by the Spirit receive new spiritual life in the present and will be raised to eternal resurrection life by the Spirit when Jesus returns.

Paul's point in the passages discussed above is clear. All people are under the sin, condemnation, and death of Adam unless they are united to the second Adam and receive the righteousness, justification, and life that are in him. These contrasts take us back to Genesis 3:15 and God's promise that the offspring of the woman would crush the head of the serpent.[23] As the second Adam, Jesus succeeded where Adam failed. In his life, death, and resurrection, Jesus has defeated sin and death, the two great enemies of

---

[19]For discussions of Jesus' role as life-giving spirit, see Richard B. Gaffin Jr., *Resurrection and Redemption: A Study in Paul's Soteriology* (Phillipsburg, NJ: P&R, 1987), 78-92, and Beale, *New Testament Biblical Theology*, 438-42.

[20]Beale, *New Testament Biblical Theology*, 583.

[21]Ridderbos, *Paul*, 56.

[22]See Vos, *Pauline Eschatology*, 168-69.

[23]Beale interprets Paul similarly when he writes, "Paul understands Jesus' resurrection as not only reversing the curse of death but also decisively defeating the devil." *New Testament Biblical Theology*, 248.

God's people. Adam brought death to humanity, but Jesus has brought life, and this life is found only through union with the risen Christ. Because Jesus has been resurrected, those who are united to him also have the hope of resurrection.

THE RESURRECTION OF JESUS AND THE NEW AGE

In the Old Testament prophetic books, the hope of restoration is connected with a renewed relationship with God in the new covenant, a return to the land, a new temple, the last-days messianic kingdom ushered in by the great son of David, and resurrection from the dead. As a result, resurrection in the age to come becomes an essential hope for God's people.

As previously discussed, the prophet Hosea highlights the close connection between Israel's restoration and resurrection hopes. In Hosea 6:1-2, Hosea calls Israel to "return to the Lord" so that the Lord will heal, bind up wounds, and revive and restore Israel, and so that God's people may live in his presence. Although resurrection is not explicit, the emphasis on God's revival of his people, God's restoration of his people, and life in God's presence strongly implies it. Notably, Hosea states that this restoration of God's people happens "on the third day," a phrase that is most likely figurative for the quick restoration of God's people. Significantly, in the New Testament there is a recurring motif that Jesus or the Messiah would be raised on the third day or after three days (see, e.g., Lk 9:22; 24:46). While the connection is not explicit, the New Testament writers most likely found in Hosea 6:1-2 a pattern of resurrection that is fulfilled, first, in Jesus and his resurrection on the third day and, second, in those who are united to Jesus and will be raised to life at the end of the age. Thus, the New Testament writers emphasize that Jesus' resurrection means that the new age has been inaugurated.

In New Testament eschatology, the kingdom age is split in two with the first and second coming of the Messiah, the new covenant unfolds with the first and second coming of Jesus, and the age of resurrection is similarly split. In describing this phenomenon, Paul contends that Christ's resurrection represents the "firstfruits," while those who are united to Christ will be raised in the future at Jesus' second coming (1 Cor 15:20-23). In this way, the resurrection of Christ is intimately bound up with the future resurrection of believers.[24] As the "firstfruits," Christ's resurrection guarantees the future resurrection of those who are united to him by faith.[25] Because Jesus has been raised to life, those who are united to Christ by faith will also in the future be raised to new life.

My focus in this book has been on the themes of creation life, death as the result of the fall, and the hope of resurrection life in redemption. The resurrection of Jesus means that the new age, the age of resurrection, has been inaugurated. While life had been promised, prophesied, and pictured in the old covenant, the resurrection of Jesus marks the beginning of the fulfillment of the curse of death being undone through resurrection life. We would be sorely mistaken if we understood Jesus' resurrection in the same way as the miracles of Old Testament prophets, Jesus, and apostles raising people from the dead. All these people who were raised from the dead eventually died again. But in his glorified bodily resurrection Jesus was raised to immortality and eternal life. The author of Hebrews emphasizes that Jesus became our exalted high priest "on the basis of the power of an indestructible life" (Heb 7:16). Jesus has been raised to eternal life, glory, and immortality, never to experience death again.

Many Jews in the first century would have readily identified Rome (or any of the nations that oppressed them throughout history) as their enemy, but they were perhaps not as quick to recognize their even greater enemies—sin and death. In order for Jesus to reign as God's Son and Messiah, he must conquer sin and death. As a result of his resurrection, Jesus has conquered these great enemies and now reigns as the Messiah and Savior of God's people. Without Jesus' resurrection, the old age of sin and death still reigns, but with his resurrection the new age of resurrection and life has been inaugurated.[26] C. S. Lewis writes,

> The New Testament writers speak as if Christ's achievement in rising from the dead was the first event of its kind in the whole history of the universe. He is the "first fruits," the "pioneer of life." He has forced open a door that has been locked since the death of the first man. He has met, fought, and beaten

---

[24]Ridderbos (*Paul*, 538) says that there is an "unbreakable unity" between Christ's resurrection and those that are united to him by faith.

[25]See Gaffin's discussions in *By Faith*, 67-74, and *Resurrection and Redemption*, 33-62.

[26]See also Gaffin, *Resurrection and Redemption*, 116.

the King of Death. Everything is different because He has done so. This is the beginning of the New Creation: a new chapter in cosmic history has opened.[27]

While death reigned in the old age, the resurrection of Jesus marks a transition to the new age, a time when death will no longer reign, but rather life through resurrection. Because Jesus has been raised, the age to come has been inaugurated and the age of resurrection has dawned.

THE RESURRECTION, ASCENSION, AND ENTHRONEMENT OF JESUS CHRIST

Not only does the resurrection serve as vindication that Jesus is the Messiah; Jesus' resurrection is also closely linked with his heavenly exaltation and enthronement at God's right hand. As we have seen, reigning with God and resurrection life are closely tied together throughout all of Scripture and redemptive history. This close relationship comes into clearer focus in the New Testament as its writers are adamant about the link between Christ's resurrection and kingship. G. K. Beale contends, "Christ's resurrection is so linked to his kingship that the two are two sides of one coin."[28] On a practical level, the New Testament writers likely noted this link between Jesus' resurrection and kingship because a dead messiah is no messiah at all. The Messiah is God's last-days king who brings victory to God's people and reigns over creation, and a dead messiah cannot fulfill this purpose. On a theological level, the Messiah had to defeat the greatest enemies of God's people—sin and death—and this happens only through the death and resurrection of Jesus. Consequently, the messianic hopes for God's people are ultimately dependent on the resurrection of Jesus.

The first four verses of Romans demonstrate this close relationship between Jesus' resurrection and kingship:

> Paul, a servant of Christ Jesus, called to be an apostle and set apart for the gospel of God—the gospel he promised beforehand through his prophets in the Holy Scriptures regarding his Son, who as to his earthly life was a descendant of David, and who through the Spirit of holiness was appointed the Son of God in power by his resurrection from the dead: Jesus Christ our Lord. (Rom 1:1-4)

---

[27]C. S. Lewis, *Miracles: A Preliminary Study* (New York: HarperSanFrancisco, 2001), 236-37.
[28]Beale, *New Testament Biblical Theology*, 247.

These verses contain much that is important for biblical theology, but here I will emphasize two things: the close connection between the gospel and the kingdom of God, and the close link between the gospel of the kingdom and Jesus' resurrection.[29]

First, Paul connects the gospel with the kingdom of God in a number of ways. To begin with, Paul is a servant of *Christ* Jesus. As previously noted, the term *Christ* is the Greek term for the Hebrew *Messiah*. Thus, Jesus Christ means Jesus the Messiah. Moreover, in the Old Testament, the "gospel" or "good news" is typically associated with God's reign. For example, Isaiah 52:7 reads,

> How beautiful on the mountains
>   are the feet of those who bring good news,
> who proclaim peace,
>   who bring good tidings,
>   who proclaim salvation,
> who say to Zion,
>   "Your God reigns!"

The "good news" in Isaiah 52:7 is that Yahweh, the God of Israel, reigns. Finally, Paul's reference to Jesus as "Son" and his description of Jesus as "a descendant of David" clearly links the gospel with the kingdom. The term *son* is a kingship term that finds its Old Testament background in God's covenant with David (2 Sam 7:14; Ps 2:7), and Paul's insistence that Jesus was a descendant of David confirms this background. According to Paul, the gospel is intimately connected with Jesus, the Old Testament Scriptures, and the kingdom of God.

Second, Paul connects the gospel of the kingdom with Jesus' resurrection. In Romans 1:4 there is a close relationship between Jesus' appointment as the Son of God in power, Jesus' resurrection from the dead, and the work of the Holy Spirit. The link between the Holy Spirit and Jesus' resurrection is significant. Just as the Spirit was instrumental in creation life (Gen 2:7), the Spirit is instrumental in resurrection life,[30] and the Spirit appoints Jesus as

---

[29]For a thorough discussion of Rom 1:3-4, its importance in redemptive history, and its significance in Romans, see Gaffin, *Resurrection and Redemption*, 98-113.
[30]In addition to Rom 1:3-4, see Eph 1:13-14, 19-20; 2:4-7; Jn 3:1-15.

the Son of God in power by his resurrection. The connection between Jesus' resurrection and his appointment as the Son of God in power is important because the resurrection of Jesus marks a new phase in his kingship.

Although Jesus is God's Son from all eternity, Lord from all eternity, and Messiah from his birth, his resurrection means that he is now the Son of God, the Messiah, and the Lord in power. In his life and sacrificial death, Jesus reigns as Lord and Messiah, but he reigns "in weakness." To be sure, Jesus always reigns, but for a time he willingly allows and gives himself to be rejected, mocked, beaten, and crucified. Yet in the midst of all of this, Jesus is still Lord and in control. Indeed, he emphasizes that no one takes his life from him, but rather he freely lays it down (Jn 10:18). Moreover, Jesus is the one who declares, "It is finished," and ultimately gives up his spirit (Jn 19:30). While in his life and sacrificial death Jesus reigns in weakness, in his resurrection he reigns as the Son of God in power. The resurrection of Jesus represents a new stage in his messianic reign. He now reigns in glory and power at the right hand of God the Father.[31]

The New Testament affirms that Jesus ascended into heaven and reigns at the right hand of God in glory and power. If Jesus has been raised to life in power as the messianic king, then he should actually be reigning. One of the stumbling blocks to faith in Jesus was that many people did not see or understand how Jesus, as the proclaimed Messiah, was reigning. In his earthly life and death, Jesus reigned in weakness and service. But after his resurrection, the question for the disciples remains! This is no doubt the impetus for the disciples' question in Acts 1:6: "Lord, are you at this time going to restore the kingdom to Israel?" This question reveals that the disciples still connect Jesus' messianic identity with his reign and the kingdom of God. Jesus is the Messiah, but how does he reign as the Messiah? For the disciples, the answer is found

---

[31]On the notion of Jesus' resurrection as a new stage in his messianic reign, see Douglas J. Moo, *The Epistle to the Romans*, New International Commentary on the New Testament (Grand Rapids, MI: Eerdmans, 1996), 47-51; Thomas R. Schreiner, *Romans*, Baker Exegetical Commentary on the New Testament (Grand Rapids, MI: Baker Academic, 1998), 39-45. On the notion of Jesus reigning "in weakness" in his sacrificial death, Leon Morris writes, "There is a sense in which Jesus was the Son of God in weakness before the resurrection but the Son of God in power thereafter," and points to 2 Cor 13:4, where Paul writes that Christ "was crucified in weakness" but now "lives by God's power." *The Epistle to the Romans*, Pillar New Testament Commentary (Grand Rapids, MI: Eerdmans, 1988), 45.

in Jesus' ascension, Jesus' heavenly enthronement, and a most important Old Testament passage.

Luke records Jesus' ascension into heaven in Luke 24:50-53 and Acts 1:9-11. With his ascension, Jesus begins his heavenly enthronement and reign. This is precisely how the disciples and New Testament writers answered the important questions of how and where Jesus presently reigns. And to arrive at this answer, they turned to the Old Testament and specifically to Psalm 110, a psalm that prophesies about a king greater than David who will reign at God's right hand over all his enemies. In Psalm 110:1-2 we read,

> The LORD says to my lord:
>
> "Sit at my right hand
>   until I make your enemies
>   a footstool for your feet."
>
> The LORD will extend your mighty scepter from Zion, saying,
>   "Rule in the midst of your enemies!"

As the Messiah, Jesus now reigns in heaven at God's right hand.

While Jesus' resurrection, ascension, and heavenly enthronement are technically distinct events, the New Testament writers move fluidly between them because they are so closely related. In Acts 2:22-36 Peter proclaims that God raised Jesus to life and subsequently exalted him to the right hand of God, citing Psalm 16 for Jesus' resurrection and Psalm 110 for his ascension and enthronement. Similarly, in his synagogue sermon, Paul proclaims that God raised Jesus from the dead and cites Psalm 2:7 ("You are my son; / today I have become your father" [Acts 13:33]), no doubt in reference to his resurrection and kingship.[32] In their respective sermons, Peter and Paul emphasize that Jesus is the final son of David and the fulfillment of the Davidic covenant. Jesus will bring the hopes, promises, and expectations of the Davidic covenant to fruition.

By appealing to Psalm 2 and Psalm 110 for Jesus' resurrection and enthronement, Peter and Paul demonstrate just how closely the New Testament community associated these events. Jesus' resurrection is his formal

---

[32]Paul also cites Is 55:3 and Ps 16:10 for Jesus' resurrection in his Acts 13 sermon.

installation and enthronement as king. In Ephesians 1:19-23 Paul alludes to this close relationship between Jesus' resurrection and heavenly enthronement when he writes that God has raised Jesus from the dead and seated him at God's right hand in the heavenly realms, where Jesus reigns over all things, both his enemies and the church. In his resurrection, Jesus the Messiah reigns in glory and power at God's right hand.

The relationship between Christ' resurrection and enthronement is so close that one event implies the other. This close relationship continues the trajectory that began in creation and continues throughout redemption: God created humanity to reign, and he created humanity for life. Although these creation purposes are lost in the fall, they are restored in redemption. The close relationship between these realities hints at an all-important truth that is often overlooked. After the fall, it is impossible to reign with God apart from resurrection. This notion is confirmed when the author of Hebrews, citing Psalm 8:4-6, emphasizes that although God has placed all things under humanity, we do not yet see all things subject to humanity (Heb 2:5-8), but "we do see Jesus . . . now crowned with glory and honor" (Heb 2:9). All of humanity does not yet reign over creation as God intended. But because of his resurrection, ascension, and exaltation, Jesus reigns over all things. Through Jesus' resurrection and enthronement, those united to Christ by faith will also in the future be raised to resurrection life to reign with him.

In his opening vision in Revelation, John sees "someone like a son of man" (Rev 1:13), and this "someone" is none other than Jesus as king in his heavenly glory and power. In the midst of John's fear, Jesus says, "Do not be afraid. I am the First and the Last. I am the Living One; I was dead, and now look, I am alive for ever and ever! And I hold the keys of death and Hades" (Rev 1:17-18). These words are astounding. Jesus affirms that he is the Lord, and he proclaims that although he was dead, he has been raised to eternal resurrection life. Moreover, as the one who has been raised from the dead and who lives and reigns forever, Jesus holds the keys of death and Hades. He is the means of salvation for others, and those who trust in him can be confident that they will also be raised to life to reign with him forever.

Why Is the Resurrection of Jesus Important?

- The resurrection serves as Jesus' vindication that he is the Messiah.

- The resurrection serves as Jesus' vindication that he is righteous and that he is God's righteous servant.

- Jesus is the second Adam who brings eschatological life and resurrection life.

- In his resurrection, Jesus ushers in the new age of life and resurrection.

- Jesus' resurrection (and subsequent ascension and enthronement) serves as Jesus' enthronement wherein he reigns in glory and power.

Figure 7.1. The significance of Jesus' resurrection

CONCLUSION AND APPLICATION

The first coming of Jesus means that the last days have begun and the new age has been inaugurated. The Old Testament prophets prophesied about a restored relationship with God through a new and better covenant, a new and greater temple, the eschatological kingdom of God ushered in by the great and final son of David, and resurrection for God's people. Jesus brings these eschatological hopes and promises to fulfillment. And as we have seen, the resurrection of Jesus is inextricably linked with these redemptive themes and eschatological hopes. This means the resurrection of Jesus is good news indeed.

First, as the perfect Son of God, Jesus is the second Adam and true Israel (Mt 3:17; Rom 5:12-21; Jn 15:1-7). God's people will be identified by their relationship to the second Adam and true Israel. In his death and resurrection, Jesus inaugurated the new covenant and accomplished full forgiveness of sins and reconciliation between God and his people (Lk 22:20; Mt 26:28; Jer 31:34; Heb 8:1-13). Significantly, Jesus' resurrection is the basis for believers' justification, and therefore the basis for a right relationship with God. Jesus has been vindicated as righteous in his resurrection, and it is only through union with the risen Christ that believers can also be declared righteous. This

is precisely the reason Paul writes that Jesus "was raised to life for our justification" (Rom 4:25).

Second, in his life Jesus represents the true and greater temple. As the
place of God's presence, Jesus has life in himself (Jn 5:26) and holds the
power of resurrection life (Jn 5:21). Although the temple of Christ's body
is destroyed with his death on the cross, Jesus' resurrection from the dead
represents the rebuilding of the temple (Jn 2:19-21). In his resurrection and
ascension, Jesus ascends to heaven and reigns at God's right hand. Through
union with Christ, believers have access to God and are seated with Christ
in the heavenly realms (Eph 2:4-6). Moreover, as the glorified temple and
"life-giving spirit" (1 Cor 15:45), Jesus pours out the Spirit on his people,
and they represent God's temple, the place of God's presence (1 Cor 3:16;
6:19; Eph 2:19-22). Jesus, as the second and greater Adam, is the source of
resurrection life for his people.

Third, as the great and final son of David and the Messiah, Jesus inaugurates
the last-days kingdom of God in his earthly life (Mk 1:15; Lk 4:14-21) and is
installed as Messiah and Lord in power in his resurrection, ascension, and
heavenly enthronement (Acts 2:32-36). Jesus has been raised to eternal, glorified, and indestructible life, and reigns at God's right hand over all things.
Those who are united to Christ by faith become a part of his eschatological
kingdom and subsequently reign with him (Eph 2:6; Rev 1:4-9).

Finally, Jesus' resurrection from the dead signifies that eschatological resurrection hopes have been inaugurated. As the "firstfruits" of the final resurrection
(1 Cor 15:20-23), Jesus' resurrection is inextricably linked with the resurrection
of his people. On the one hand, those who are united to Christ by faith are
already made alive in Christ and raised up with him through spiritual resurrection (Eph 2:4-6). On the other hand, Christ's resurrection ensures the future
bodily resurrection of his people at his second coming (1 Cor 15:23).[33]

---

[33]In *Resurrection and Redemption*, Richard Gaffin argues that Jesus' resurrection serves as his
justification (vindication), adoption (appointment as the Son of God in power), sanctification
(freedom from the power of death), and glorification (glorified bodily resurrection). Because
believers are united to the risen Christ and because they are indwelled by the Spirit, they also
receive justification, adoption, sanctification, and glorification. For Gaffin's full discussion, see
Resurrection and Redemption, 77-134, esp. 114-34.

Table 7.1. Jesus' resurrection and redemption of God's people

THE RESURRECTION OF JESUS	REDEMPTION FOR JESUS' PEOPLE
Jesus vindicated as righteous	Believers justified through Christ's resurrection (Rom 4:25)
Resurrected Jesus as rebuilt and glorified temple; ascended Jesus at right hand of God	Believers/church as the temple (1 Cor 3:16; 6:19; Eph 2:19-22); believers seated in the heavenly realms in Christ (Eph 2:6)
Resurrection as Jesus' enthronement	Believers reign with Christ (Eph 2:4-6; Rev 1:4-9)
Jesus' resurrection as "firstfruits"	Spiritual resurrection in the present (Eph 2:4-6); future bodily resurrection of Christ's people (1 Cor 15:23)

John Stott has referred to Christianity as a "rescue religion,"[34] and the hero, the one who rescues his people, is the one that Christianity is named after—Jesus Christ. While the reign of Adam is marked by sin, condemnation, and death, with Jesus' resurrection the new age of righteousness, justification, and resurrection life has begun. As N. T. Wright notes, the resurrection of Jesus represents "the beginning of that new life, the fresh grass growing through concrete of corruption and decay in the old world."[35] The resurrection of Jesus changes everything—it changes our present and it changes our future. It provides the impetus to continue in faith and to trust God that he will complete his plan of redemption. God has rescued Jesus from death, and Jesus reigns in glory and power. That is also our hope. Since Christians are united to Christ by faith, they can be confident that God will rescue them from sin and death and raise them up for eternal resurrection life. Although we still look forward to that future reality, Jesus' resurrection and the life-giving presence of the Spirit guarantee that our hope will be realized.

---

[34]John Stott, *Basic Christianity* (Downers Grove, IL: InterVarsity Press, 2008), 111.
[35]Wright, *Surprised by Hope*, 123.

Chapter Eight

THE CHURCH RAISED
TO NEW LIFE

Love that will not betray you, dismay or enslave you.
It will set you free,
Be more like the man you were made to be.

MUMFORD AND SONS

IN THE PREVIOUS TWO CHAPTERS, I discussed how the first coming of Jesus, represented in his life, death, and resurrection, is essential for God's resurrection purposes. In this chapter, I turn my attention to the church age. Although the term *church* can be used in different ways, I use the term here as a reference to the universal church—all God's people who are united to Christ by faith. Bible scholars often refer to the time between the first and second coming of Jesus as a time of inaugurated eschatology. Jesus has inaugurated the last-days kingdom of God in his first coming, but it will not be consummated until his second coming. The age of resurrection has dawned with Jesus' resurrection, but believers look forward to their future resurrection when Christ returns. This period between the first and second coming of Jesus represents the age of the church.

The church age represents a time of inaugurated eschatology because believers are united to the risen and exalted Lord Jesus. In Ephesians 1:3 Paul writes that God "has blessed us in the heavenly realms with every spiritual blessing in Christ." But the blessings that God has bestowed in Christ and by the Spirit have not yet reached their final fulfillment. Scholars often refer to this experience as the "already" and "not yet" because these blessings of salvation have already been inaugurated but they have not yet been consummated. In this chapter, I will discuss how God's work of salvation continues to unfold in this time between the first and second coming of Jesus. Special attention will be given to how God's promise to bring resurrection life to his people unfolds and is fulfilled in the age of the church.

RESTORED RELATIONSHIP WITH GOD

Through the life, death, and resurrection of Jesus, believers enjoy a restored relationship with God. This is evident throughout the New Testament. Jesus is the only way to God (Jn 14:6), Jesus is the only mediator between God and people (1 Tim 2:5), and salvation is found in no other name but Jesus (Acts 4:12). In communicating this restored relationship with God, the Bible uses many different descriptions. For example, those who were formerly alienated from God are now *reconciled* to him through Christ (Col 1:21-22; Rom 5:9-11; 2 Cor 5:16-20). Those who were formerly outside God's family have been *adopted* into his family (Rom 8:14-17).

One important and frequently used description of salvation is *justification*. The biblical doctrine of justification is that believers are forgiven of their sin and declared righteous before God through faith in Jesus.[1] As we have seen, there is a close connection throughout Scripture between a restored relationship with God and resurrection hopes. This is because a right relationship with God is the basis for life. In Romans 5, after his argument for justification by faith, Paul discusses the implications and consequences of justification. He moves seamlessly between the *justification* of believers and the new *life* that they have in Christ (see Rom 5:12-21). This is because one implies the other. Whereas Adam's disobedience and sin brought condemnation and death to humanity, Jesus' perfect righteousness brings justification and life to those united to Christ by faith.

---

[1]The Westminster Shorter Catechism (question 33) defines justification as "an act of God's free grace, wherein he (pardons) all our sins, and (accepts) us as righteous in his sight, only for the righteousness of Christ imputed to us, and received by faith alone."

Jesus' vindication goes hand in hand with his resurrection, and Scripture reveals the same is true for believers. There is a close connection between believers' justification and their resurrection. On the one hand, those who have been justified are raised to new life in the Spirit now. This is Paul's point in Romans 6 when, on the heels of his argument for justification by faith, he emphasizes that Christ's resurrection means that believers are also raised to new life (Rom 6:1-14). Similarly, in Ephesians 2:1-6 Paul says that God has made believers, who were previously dead in sin and at enmity with God, "alive with Christ." In these passages, Paul highlights the close connection between a restored relationship with God and new spiritual life, or what we could term "spiritual resurrection." These two realities are so closely linked that one implies the other. The result of justification and a restored relationship with God is "eternal life through Jesus Christ our Lord" (Rom 5:21). This eternal life has been inaugurated in the present but will only be consummated in the future with bodily resurrection.

LIFE IN GOD'S PRESENCE

The New Testament highlights some important ways that believers experience God's life-giving presence. As the "last Adam" and the "life-giving spirit" (1 Cor 15:45), Jesus poured out the Holy Spirit after his ascension into heaven. The coming of the Spirit at Pentecost is marked by three significant signs: the blowing of a violent wind from heaven, tongues of fire resting on believers, and speaking in other tongues.

First, the blowing of the violent wind from heaven sets apart Pentecost as a new-creation event. God breathed life into Adam at creation, and God called breath to enter the dead bones in order to give them life in Ezekiel 37. At Pentecost, the coming of the Spirit represents a fulfillment of this new-creation hope and prophecy.

Second, throughout the Bible, fire often represents God's presence.[2] The tongues of fire over the heads of Jesus' disciples are a visible demonstration that God now dwells with his people through the Spirit. Here we should recall that Jesus represents the temple in his first coming. With his

---

[2]See, e.g., Gen 15:17; Ex 3:1-6; 13:21; 19:18; 40:34-38; Deut 4:24; Lk 3:16-17; Heb 12:18.

resurrection, the temple of Jesus' body is restored and raised in power. After his ascension, Jesus pours out his Spirit, and those who are indwelled by the Spirit of Christ are the body of Christ and the temple. This reality represents the fulfillment of Jesus' promise to the Samaritan woman that "a time is coming when you will worship the Father neither on this mountain nor in Jerusalem" (Jn 4:21) because "his worshipers must worship in the Spirit and in truth" (Jn 4:24). Because God dwells with his people through his Spirit, they no longer need to go to a physical temple. Paul insists that believers represent the temple and God's presence on the earth in this period of redemptive history (1 Cor 3:16; 6:19; Eph 2:19-22). Rather than the physical temple, the church, composed of all believers, is now the place where God chooses to dwell.

The third sign, speaking in tongues, also represents an important eschatological reality. As a reversal of God's judgment at the Tower of Babel, the apostolic community is enabled to proclaim the gospel to the Jews who were gathered from all over the world in their own languages, beginning the fulfillment of God's plan to bring salvation to the ends of the earth.

As a result of the indwelling of the Spirit, those who are united to Christ receive an even greater experience of God's presence than Old Testament believers who worshiped the Lord in the temple. In one sense, the dilemma and angst of the psalmist in Psalm 84 is no longer applicable to the new-covenant believer. The psalmist writes,

> How lovely is your dwelling place,
>   Lord Almighty!
> My soul yearns, even faints,
>   for the courts of the Lord;
> my heart and my flesh cry out
>   for the living God. (Ps 84:1-2)

When he considers the glory and importance of the temple, the psalmist confesses that he is jealous of the sparrow who has a home near the temple (Ps 84:3).[3] The intimacy of dwelling with the Lord in the temple

---

[3]In another sense, the longing of Ps 84 is still applicable because believers long for the consummation of God's life-giving presence, which will be experienced only in the final temple of the new creation.

in the old covenant is surpassed by the new-covenant experience of God dwelling with his people by his Spirit. New-covenant believers need not worship in a certain place, because they worship "in the Spirit and in truth" (Jn 4:24).

Throughout Scripture, God's presence is closely connected with the hope of resurrection life. The new-covenant experience of God dwelling with his people by the Spirit continues this trajectory. Paul insists that the Spirit is the "deposit" that guarantees the future inheritance and redemption of believers (Eph 1:13-14). In Romans 8:11 he writes, "If the Spirit of him who raised Jesus from the dead is living in you, he who raised Christ from the dead will also give life to your mortal bodies because of his Spirit who lives in you." This means that the new life in Christ is both a present and a future reality. Just as God raised Jesus from the dead, he has also raised Christians from their spiritual death to new spiritual life (Eph 2:1-10). The Spirit who gives new life to believers in the present is the same Spirit who will bring to completion the future inheritance of believers in bodily resurrection when Jesus returns.

In addition to the indwelling of the Spirit, union with the ascended Christ highlights believers' present experience of God's presence. Just as Jesus was raised from the dead and is now in God's presence (Eph 1:19-20), so also those who are "in Christ" have been made alive by God, raised with Christ, and seated with Christ in the heavenly realms in Christ Jesus (Eph 2:5-6). New-covenant believers experience God's presence through the indwelling of the Holy Spirit and through their union with Christ. These realities reflect the new life that is associated with God's presence and reveal the close connection between God's presence and life.

REIGNING WITH GOD

In his first coming, represented in his life, death, and resurrection, Jesus inaugurated the last-days kingdom of God. In Mark 1:15 Jesus proclaims, "The time has come. . . . The kingdom of God has come near. Repent and believe the good news!" Not only does Jesus draw a clear connection between the gospel and the kingdom; he communicates the appropriate response to the inbreaking of the kingdom of God: repentance and belief. In the age of the church, the same call to repentance is operative. In his Pentecost sermon, Peter proclaims that God has made Jesus both Lord and Messiah (Acts 2:36), and exhorts his hearers to "repent and be baptized" (Acts 2:38). Similarly, in Acts 3:19-20 Peter proclaims, "Repent, then, and turn to God, so that your sins may be wiped out, that times of refreshing may come from the Lord, and that he may send the Messiah, who has been appointed for you— even Jesus." Here Peter connects repentance with forgiveness and times of refreshing in the present age, and with the second coming of Jesus in the future.

Although only a small sample, these passages demonstrate that the kingdom of God has been inaugurated with Jesus' first coming and that people can join and participate in the eschatological kingdom through repentance and faith. Indeed, Peter makes it clear that all who come to Christ in repentance and faith, whether Jew or Gentile, are God's chosen people and his kingdom (royal priesthood) (1 Pet 2:9-10). While this blessing was largely restricted to Israel in the old covenant (Ex 19:4-6), the new covenant means the fulfillment of the promises and prophecies of the worldwide eschatological kingdom of God. Moreover, as Paul emphasizes, salvation is nothing less than being rescued from Satan and his dominion and being brought into the kingdom of Christ, through whom believers have received redemption and forgiveness of sins (Col 1:13-14).

THE PRESENT RESURRECTION OF BELIEVERS

As a result of Jesus' life, death, and resurrection, believers have been restored to a right relationship with God, experience God's presence through the indwelling of the Holy Spirit, and have become a part of God's last-days kingdom. In light of this, it should not come as a surprise that the New Testament speaks of a present resurrection for believers. When Christians think about resurrection, they usually think of it as a future event, but it is important to realize that those who are united to Christ already experience the beginning of resurrection life through the Holy Spirit.

Inaugurated Eschatology: Salvation "Already" Accomplished and Experienced

- Reconciliation with God / justification (forgiven of sin and declared righteous before God)

- Life in God's presence through the indwelling of the Holy Spirit and through union with Christ; believers/church as the temple

- Brought into God's kingdom; reign with Christ

- Raised up with Christ (Eph 2:4-6); new-creation life (Eph 4:22-24; 2:10); resurrection life through spiritual resurrection (Eph 2:1-6)

Figure 8.1. Salvation already realized

In several places the Gospel of John hints at or directly teaches a present resurrection for believers. In the prologue, John takes us back to creation to demonstrate that there is a new creation in Jesus. Just as God gave life in creation, he gives new life in new creation. Indeed, faith in Jesus leads to new birth and becoming children of God (Jn 1:12-13). What John implies in many places is explicit in John 5:24-25 when Jesus proclaims, "Very truly I tell you, whoever hears my word and believes him who sent me has eternal life and will not be judged but has crossed over from death to life. Very truly I tell you, a time is coming and has now come when the dead will hear the voice of the Son of God and those who hear will live."[4] Whoever trusts in Jesus has already crossed over from death to life. As a result, the possession and experience of resurrection life has already begun.

In his letters, Paul frequently emphasizes that resurrection life has already been inaugurated for believers.[5] As a result of being crucified with Christ, he states that he no longer lives but rather Christ lives in him (Gal 2:20). When believers are united to Christ, his death becomes their death and his resurrection becomes their resurrection. Because the risen

---

[4]See also 1 Jn 3:14.

[5]See, e.g., Eph 2:5-6; Col 2:12-13; 3:1; Rom 6:4-13; Gal 2:20. Richard B. Gaffin Jr. highlights these references in *By Faith, Not by Sight: Paul and the Order of Salvation*, 2nd ed. (Phillipsburg, NJ: P&R, 2013), 71.

Christ lives in believers, resurrection life has already begun. This also reflects Paul's train of thought in Romans 6:1-14 when he writes that Christ's resurrection means that believers are called and enabled to live new lives. In Colossians and Ephesians, Paul often stresses the realized aspects of salvation and, in striking fashion, writes that believers have been made alive with Christ and raised up with Christ.[6] As Richard Gaffin notes, this present resurrection is an essential element in Pauline soteriology and should be understood not merely as metaphorical but as "a realistic description of the event that inaugurates individual Christian experience."[7] The bodily resurrection of believers is still in the future, but the present spiritual (of the Holy Spirit) resurrection anticipates and guarantees that future final resurrection.[8]

Ephesians 2:1-10 is perhaps the most famous passage on salvation in Christ. For our purposes, the passage demonstrates not only that resurrection life is a present reality for believers but also that this experience of present resurrection is connected with the other redemptive themes we have traced. This is of central importance because, in the history of redemption, resurrection hopes are always linked with a right relationship with God, God's presence, and reigning with God.

Ephesians 2:1-10 is likely familiar because of the emphasis on salvation by grace through faith, but what should not be missed is the clear movement from death to life. In the preceding passage, Paul highlights Jesus' movement from death to resurrection life. In Ephesians 1:19-23 Paul writes that God's great power has raised Christ from the dead and seated him at God's right hand in the heavenly realms. The movement is from Christ's physical death to Christ's bodily resurrection to his heavenly enthronement at the right hand of God. In Ephesians 2:1-10 Paul writes that this same movement is true

---

[6]See Col 2:12-13; 3:1-4; Eph 2:4-6. I will discuss Eph 2:1-10 in more detail below.

[7]Richard B. Gaffin Jr., *Resurrection and Redemption: A Study in Paul's Soteriology* (Phillipsburg, NJ: P&R, 1987), 59.

[8]Recall here Ezekiel's vision of the valley of dry bones, where spiritual renewal is depicted by resurrection language and implies future bodily resurrection. See, e.g., Eph 1:13-14, where Paul writes that the Spirit is the "guarantee" of believers' inheritance. On this reality, see Geerhardus Vos, "The Eschatological Aspect of the Pauline Conception of the Spirit," in *Biblical and Theological Studies* (New York: Charles Scribner's Sons, 1912), 209-59.

for those who are united to Christ by faith, but his emphasis is spiritual death to spiritual life.

An outline of Ephesians 2:1-10 includes three basic sections: (1) pre-Christian past (dead in sin) (Eph 2:1-3); (2) new life in Christ (Eph 2:4-7); (3) faith, works, and new life in Christ (Eph 2:8-10). In Paul's description of believers' movement from death to life, he connects all the redemptive themes we have traced. First, believers have a restored relationship with God. Although Paul does not use justification language, he describes believers before being saved by Christ as those who were dead in sin, lived in the ways of the world, followed Satan, lived by the sinful nature, and were deserving of God's wrath (Eph 2:1-3). As a result of Christ's work, they are now saved by grace and are newly created to walk in good works (as opposed to the ways of the world and the sinful nature) (Eph 2:8-10). This change also comes into focus in the next passage when Paul describes believers as "fellow citizens with God's people and also members of his household" (Eph 2:19).

Second, since God has seated believers in the heavenly realms (Eph 2:6), they have been ushered into God's presence through union with Christ. Jesus is seated at God's right hand in the heavenly realms (Eph 1:20), and those who are united to Christ are seated with Christ in heaven. Moreover, the indwelling of the Spirit in believers (Eph 1:13-14) and the description of the church as the temple (Eph 2:19-22) are consistent with the new-covenant reality of God dwelling with his people by his Spirit. Thus, believers have access to God through the Spirit and through their union with Christ.

Third, Paul emphasizes that believers *already* participate in reigning with God. Ever since the fall, when Adam and Eve chose to submit to the word of the serpent, all of humanity has been aligned with one of two camps: the offspring of the woman or the offspring of the serpent. Paul makes it clear that before Christ people are separated from God, are allied with the serpent, and actually follow and serve Satan (Eph 2:2). But this is not the case for believers. Through his resurrection, ascension, and heavenly enthronement, Jesus fulfills Psalm 110 and reigns at God's right hand over all his enemies and the church (Eph 1:20-23). Because of God's grace and on account of their union with Christ, believers also participate in Christ's reign and are now seated with Christ in the heavenly realms (Eph 2:6). Heaven represents the place of God's reign and the place where Christ reigns, yet believers have become a part of God's kingdom and already participate in Christ's reign, even in their earthly lives.

With the good news that believers have a restored relationship with God, have access to God's presence through union with Christ, and participate in Christ's reign, it should not be surprising that Paul says that believers have been raised to life. In Ephesians 1:19-23 the movement was from Christ's death to Christ's resurrection to Christ's reign. In Ephesians 2:1-10 believers are brought from death to life to enthronement with Christ. The movements are the same because the same power that raised Christ from the dead is also at work in believers (Eph 1:19).

But while the direction of the movement is the same for Christ and believers, the connotation is different. Jesus was raised from physical death to bodily resurrection, but believers have been raised from spiritual death to spiritual resurrection. Whereas they were formerly dead in sin, God has made believers alive in Christ and raised them up with Christ. Indeed, they are also newly created in Christ with a new orientation in life (Eph 2:10). In Ephesians 2:1-10 Paul makes it clear that believers have already been raised spiritually to new life in Christ, that believers have already inherited spiritual resurrection. This is of utmost importance because the presence and work of the Spirit is the "deposit" of believers' future inheritance and redemption (Eph 1:13-14) and the basis for the new life in Christ that believers are called to live out (Rom 8:5-17; Gal 5:13-26; Eph 4:20-24; 5:18).

A second passage, John 3:1-36, also highlights the present resurrection life of believers and its close connection with the themes we have traced. In his conversation with Nicodemus, Jesus tells Nicodemus that he must be "born again"[9] to be a part of the kingdom of God. For Nicodemus, a

---

[9]The Greek term for "again" can be translated as "again" or "from above." Nicodemus understands the term as "again" (see Jn 3:4), but Jesus makes it clear that Nicodemus' understanding is quite lacking. Regardless, both senses are true. To be born again is to be born of God or born from above, and to be born from above is to receive a second birth.

Pharisee and a member of the Jewish ruling council, the ultimate hope was God's reign coming to earth in the eschatological kingdom ushered in by the Messiah. For people to be part of this eschatological kingdom, they must be born again, a clear reference to new life. Here the connection between reigning with God and resurrection comes into focus. Nicodemus misunderstands Jesus' meaning, and Jesus clarifies that to be born again is to be "born of water and the Spirit" (Jn 3:5). The reference to the new birth from the Spirit should undoubtedly be understood as new-creation life. This is confirmed when Jesus provides a clear contrast between earthly life and new-creation life and proclaims, "Flesh gives birth to flesh, but the Spirit gives birth to spirit" (Jn 3:6). In light of the Spirit's connection with new life and God's presence (Jn 4:23-24), the close link between resurrection and God's presence comes into focus.

John goes on to emphasize that eternal life is through faith in Christ (Jn 3:15-16). The way he describes salvation and eternal life is significant. On the one hand, there is a clear connection in John 3:17-18 between eternal life and a right relationship with God: "For God did not send his Son into the world to condemn the world, but to save the world through him. Whoever believes in him is not condemned." Those who believe in Jesus are in a right relationship with God and are therefore not condemned. On the other hand, John makes it clear that faith in Jesus means salvation from death ("shall not perish") and eternal life (Jn 3:16). He highlights these themes again when he writes, "Whoever believes in the Son has eternal life, but whoever rejects the Son will not see life, for God's wrath remains on them" (Jn 3:36). Faith in Jesus leads to a right relationship with God and eternal life. To summarize this discussion of John 3, the hope of eternal and new-creation life undergirds Jesus' entire conversation with Nicodemus. This hope is closely connected to reigning with God, God's presence, and a right relationship with God.[10]

---

[10]G. K. Beale, in his discussion of Jn 3, similarly equates being "born again" with resurrection and identifies the close connection between resurrection life and the kingdom of God; see *A New Testament Biblical Theology: The Unfolding of the Old Testament in the New* (Grand Rapids, MI: Baker Academic, 2011), 235-37.

Table 8.1. Present resurrection of believers

REDEMPTIVE THEME	EPHESIANS 2:1-10	JOHN 3:1-36
Relationship with God	Saved by grace (2:8-9)	Saved; not condemned (3:17-18)
God's presence	Seated with Christ in heaven (2:6)	New birth by the Spirit (3:5-6)
Reigning with God	Seated/reign with Christ in heaven (2:6)	Brought into the kingdom (3:3-5)
Present resurrection	Made alive in Christ / raised up (2:5-6)	Saved from death (3:16); eternal life (3:16); new birth (3:3-7)

THE "ALREADY" AND "NOT YET" CHARACTER OF REDEMPTION

In this chapter, my emphasis has been on the aspects of salvation that are already realized in Christ. As a result of Christ' work, believers have a restored relationship with God, have access to God's presence, are a part of the kingdom of God, and have resurrection life. But although salvation has been inaugurated, it has not yet been consummated. I will reserve my discussion of the future elements of redemption for the next chapter, but I would be remiss if I did not mention here the eschatological tension of salvation that believers experience in this life.

First, although believers have been justified (i.e., forgiven and declared righteous), they look forward to the day when they will be openly vindicated and when they will be set free from the presence of sin. Second, although Christians have access to God's presence through Christ's work and through the Spirit, at Christ's second coming the entirety of the new creation will be God's dwelling place, and believers will have more immediate access to God's presence. Third, believers have been brought into God's kingdom and participate in his reign, but since they await the consummation of the kingdom with Jesus' second coming, they continue to experience suffering, trial, and persecution. Only in the future will believers reign with Christ in power—without sin, without suffering, without persecution, and with all of God's enemies defeated. Finally, there are both realized and future aspects to believers' resurrection. In reference to the "inner man," the believer is already raised, but in reference to the "outer man," the believer still awaits his or her future resurrection.[11] Thus, believers have been raised to new spiritual life, but they await their future bodily and glorified resurrection.

Table 8.2. Eschatological tension

ALREADY / PRESENT	NOT YET / FUTURE
Reconciliation with God / justification	Open vindication; free from the presence of sin
Indwelling of the Spirit and union with Christ	Life in God's presence in new creation
Brought into God's kingdom; reign with Christ	Reign with Christ in power; God's enemies defeated
Spiritual resurrection	Glorified bodily resurrection

What should be evident is how closely related these redemptive themes are throughout all of Scripture. Richard Gaffin highlights the close connection between resurrection and justification in light of their present and future aspects when he writes, "Relating that forensic dimension to the already-not yet structure of the resurrection, then, leads to this conclusion: as believers are already raised with Christ, they have been justified; as they are not yet resurrected, they are still to be justified."[12] Gaffin explains that there are both present and future aspects to resurrection and justification, and these aspects have a corresponding relationship. These categories of justification and resurrection correspond to two of the redemptive themes we have traced—a right relationship with God and life.

This "already/not yet" tension is true for all God's redemptive purposes. Insofar as believers are resurrected, they are in a right relationship with God (justified), they reign with God, and they have life in God's presence. Insofar as believers have not been resurrected, they await justification, life in God's presence, and reigning with God. The close connections between these realities have not received their due attention in biblical studies, especially the

---

[11]Gaffin, *By Faith*, 74; see also Geerhardus Vos, *The Pauline Eschatology* (1930; repr., Phillipsburg, NJ: P&R, 1994), 204-5.

[12]Gaffin, *By Faith*, 99. Gaffin (*Resurrection and Redemption*, 127-34) also emphasizes the close relationship between believers' resurrection and their justification, adoption, sanctification, and glorification.

connection between resurrection and reigning with God. For example, on the one hand, in Ephesians 2:4-6 believers have *already* been raised with Christ, and they correspondingly *already* reign with Christ. On the other hand, when Paul references the future bodily resurrection in 1 Corinthians 15:35-58, reigning with God is also in the future (see also 1 Cor 4:8). In light of this, we could even say that believers reign with God if they have been resurrected, while they do not reign with God if they have not been resurrected. We will continue to explore the relationships between these redemptive themes in the next chapter.

CONCLUSION AND APPLICATION

The hope of resurrection is not a random development in Scripture or in the history of redemption. Rather, it can be traced back to God's promise in Genesis 3:15 that the offspring of the woman would crush the head of the serpent. With the first coming of Jesus, we are introduced to the serpent-crusher who accomplishes salvation. He is the second Adam who succeeds where Adam failed, and he is the Son of God, the messianic king, and the Savior. For those who are united to Christ, salvation has been inaugurated but it has not yet been consummated. This means that believers live in a strange time indeed, a time between the ages, a time between the first and second coming of Jesus. In light of this, I will offer some application thoughts that are directly connected to the redemptive themes we have traced, with special attention to God's work of resurrection in the life of believers. Since this topic has often been neglected, this application section will be lengthier than the others.

First, because believers have been justified through faith in Christ, all their sins—past, present, and future—have been forgiven, and they no longer stand condemned before God (Rom 8:1). But in this time between the ages, believers still struggle with sin (see Rom 7:14-25).[13] Because believers will not be set free from the presence of sin in this life, they are given the promise not only of forgiveness in justification but also of forgiveness in sanctification. First John 1:9 reads, "If we confess our sins, he is faithful and just and will

---

[13]Although the interpretation is debated, I lean toward understanding Rom 7:14-25 as Paul's personal and post-Christian experience.

forgive us our sins and purify us from all unrighteousness." This promise applies not only to the "once and for all" forgiveness in justification but also to the ongoing forgiveness in sanctification.

Psalm 32 is a noteworthy illustration of the promise of forgiveness in both justification and sanctification. As Paul shows us, Psalm 32:1-2 provides a good Old Testament example of justification by faith (see Rom 4:7-8), but David's life experience recounted in the psalm also illustrates the freedom of forgiveness in sanctification through confession of sin. David recalls,

> When I kept silent,
>   my bones wasted away
>   through my groaning all day long.
> For day and night
>   your hand was heavy on me;
> my strength was sapped
>   as in the heat of summer.
>
> Then I acknowledged my sin to you
>   and did not cover up my iniquity.
> I said, "I will confess
>   my transgressions to the LORD."
> And you forgave
>   the guilt of my sin. (Ps 32:3-5)

To confess our sins is to find forgiveness and freedom and to be restored experientially in our relationship with God (in sanctification).

Second, through faith in Jesus, believers experience God's life-giving presence through the indwelling of the Spirit and through union with Christ. The New Testament makes it clear that believers have access to God through faith in Christ (Jn 14:6; Col 3:1-4; Eph 2:6; Heb 10:19-22). Still, Christians look forward to a greater experience of God's presence in the future, which will come only when God's life-giving presence permeates the entirety of the new creation. In the time between the ages, the author of Hebrews exhorts us to "draw near to God with a sincere heart and with the full assurance that faith brings" (Heb 10:22), and Paul writes that we are to approach God "with freedom and confidence" through Christ (Eph 3:12). So the present experience of God's life-giving presence is also a call to action. Because we have access to God through Christ, we should be ready and willing to come to him for forgiveness, worship, thanksgiving, strength, and peace.

Third, through repentance and faith, believers are a part of the eschatological kingdom of God (Mk 1:15; Acts 3:19-20). Through union with Christ, they also participate in Christ's present reign (Eph 2:6). But because Jesus has not yet returned and the eschatological kingdom of God has not yet been consummated, believers continue to experience suffering, persecution, and failure in this time between the ages. As Revelation 1:9 indicates, this is a time not only of "kingdom" but also of "suffering" and "patient endurance." We look forward to the time when we will reign with Christ over the new creation without sin and suffering. In this time between the ages, Jesus exhorts his followers to "seek first [God's] kingdom and his righteousness" (Mt 6:33). So we see again that to be a participant in the kingdom of God is also a call to action. We are to orient our lives around the kingdom and around God's priorities, and we are called to be a part of extending God's kingdom to the ends of the earth (Acts 1:6-8).

Finally, in light of a restored relationship with God, access to God's presence, and participation in the kingdom of God, resurrection life has begun.[14] Since Jesus has been raised from the dead and since believers have been spiritually raised, the age of resurrection has been inaugurated. Whereas they were previously dead in sin, through union with Christ and through the indwelling of the Spirit, God has made believers alive in Christ and they have been raised up spiritually. This means that "the Christian life is resurrection life."[15] This new reality has major implications for believers. In fact, the very reason that Paul and the other New Testament authors give commands and exhortations for obedience is that God has made believers alive in Christ.

In Romans 6 Paul outlines the implications of Christ's death and resurrection for believers. Although bodily resurrection is in the future (Rom 6:5, 8),

---

[14]On the "mysterious" nature of eschatological resurrection unfolding through the different stages of Christ's resurrection, believers' spiritual resurrection, and the future bodily resurrection of believers, see G. K. Beale and Benjamin L. Gladd, *Hidden but Now Revealed: A Biblical Theology of Mystery* (Downers Grove, IL: IVP Academic, 2014), 288-91.

[15]Gaffin, *By Faith*, 77.

believers have died to sin, are no longer slaves to sin, and have been set free from sin for a purpose—so that they might live a new life (Rom 6:2-10). On account of their union with Christ and God's work in their lives, believers should "count [themselves] dead to sin but alive to God in Christ Jesus" (Rom 6:11). As those who have been brought from death to life, believers are to offer themselves to God as instruments of righteousness (Rom 6:13). Similarly, in Ephesians 4:22-24 Paul writes that believers are to "put off" the old self and "put on the new self, created to be like God in true righteousness and holiness."[16]

Paul's point is clear. Because believers have been brought from death to life and have been newly created in Christ, they are to live in light of that new reality. The new resurrection life that believers have received in Christ is the foundation for obedience and sanctification.[17] In this sense, believers are to "be who they are" or to "become what they are" in Christ.[18] Those who have been brought from death to life no longer live for sin or according to the old person, because Christ's transforming work has made them alive and has changed their lives.

The dawning of the new age also means that the age of the Spirit has begun. The coming of the Holy Spirit represents the fulfillment of numerous Old Testament prophecies (Jer 31:31-34; Ezek 11:19-20; 36:24-27; 37:14; Joel 2:28). As in all aspects of redemption, there is an "already/not yet" tension in the new life in the Spirit. As the seal and deposit, the Spirit guarantees the future redemption of God's people (Eph 1:13-14). In the fullness of the age to come and in the consummation of salvation, believers will be animated by God's Spirit to the extent that they no longer sin. Moreover, the entirety of the new creation will be God's temple and will be filled with God's life-giving presence (Ezek 37:27; Hab 2:14; Rev 11:15; 21:1-5, 22-27). But in this time between the ages, believers are called to "walk by the Spirit" (Gal 5:16), to "live by the Spirit" (Gal 5:25), to "keep in step with the Spirit" (Gal 5:25), and to "be filled with the Spirit" (Eph 5:18).

---

[16]The grammar here is difficult, since the infinitives can function as either imperatives or indicatives. In either case, Paul emphasizes the new resurrection reality for believers.

[17]See Thomas R. Schreiner, *Paul: Apostle of God's Glory in Christ* (Downers Grove, IL: IVP Academic, 2001), 257-61.

[18]Gaffin uses similar language in *By Faith*, 80.

What should not be missed is the close connection between new resurrection life and the Christian life in the power of the Holy Spirit.[19] The Spirit is instrumental in creation life, in Jesus' resurrection, in the future bodily resurrection of believers, and here in new spiritual resurrection life. The same power that raised Christ from the dead is also at work in believers (Eph 1:18-20), and this is nothing less than the Spirit's resurrection power.[20] Although it would be misguided to completely conflate the new resurrection life of believers and the Christian life in the power of the Spirit, they nevertheless refer to the same reality. Christians are often confounded when they contemplate what is meant by the biblical command to walk or live by the Spirit. When we connect life in the power of the Spirit with new resurrection life, we catch a glimpse of what this means. In both instances, the Spirit-empowered life and new resurrection life give Christians the power and ability to obey God's commands and live out the Christian life.[21]

As in all aspects of redemption, this new resurrection life has an eschatological tension. Although believers still struggle with ongoing sin, they are now nevertheless indwelled by the Spirit, created anew, and raised to new life in Christ. In light of this reality, they can walk in good works (Eph 2:10), sow to please the Spirit (Gal 6:8), live by the Spirit (Rom 8:5, 13; Gal 5:16, 25), and live a life worthy of their calling (Eph 4:1). All of this emphasizes the "practicality of inaugurated eschatology for Christian living."[22] Because believers have been raised to new life and because they have been given the Spirit, they can walk in God's commands and glorify him in their lives, albeit imperfectly. In the fullness of the new creation, God's word will be completely written on the hearts and minds of his people, who will be completely dominated by the Spirit. Only then will God's people no longer sin and be perfectly obedient to God's word and commands.

---

[19]See also the discussions of Herman Ridderbos, *Paul: An Outline of His Theology*, trans. John Richard de Witt (Grand Rapids, MI: Eerdmans, 1975), 214-23; Beale, *New Testament Biblical Theology*, 251, 276, 308, 835-70; Gaffin, *By Faith*, 85; Sam Allberry, *Lifted: Experiencing the Resurrection Life* (Phillipsburg, NJ: P&R, 2010), 67-73.

[20]Vos (*Pauline Eschatology*, 163-66) identifies the Spirit as the source (both the creator and sustainer) of believers' resurrection life.

[21]See Beale, *New Testament Biblical Theology*, 251, 308, 836.

[22]Beale, *New Testament Biblical Theology*, 865.

Table 8.3. Eschatological tension and application for Christian life

ALREADY / PRESENT	NOT YET / FUTURE	PRESENT APPLICATION
Reconciliation with God / justification	Open vindication; free from the presence of sin	Promise of ongoing forgiveness in sanctification; blessing of forgiveness through confession (1 Jn 1:9)
Indwelling of the Spirit and union with Christ	Life in God's presence in new creation	Draw near to God (Heb 10:22) / approach God with freedom and confidence (Eph 3:12)
Brought into God's kingdom; reign with Christ	Reign with Christ in power; God's enemies defeated	Seek first the kingdom of God (Mt 6:33) / kingdom work; Great Commission (Mt 28:18-20; Acts 1:8)
Resurrection life through spiritual resurrection	Glorified bodily resurrection	Live in light of resurrection life and new spiritual life (Rom 6:1-14; Eph 4:22-24); become who you are in Christ

In one of my favorite songs, "Sigh No More," the band Mumford and Sons sings about a love that does not enslave us but rather sets us free to be the people that we were created to be. Regardless of the band's intention, the lyrics provide a powerful picture of how a restored relationship with God changes us, renews us, and makes us alive in Christ. Because of God's love for us in Christ, we have been set free from our slavery to sin (Rom 6:18) and newly created (2 Cor 5:17; Eph 2:10; 4:22-24) to be more like the men and women God created us to be. This is the wonderful news of the gospel. Not only have we been forgiven of sin and declared righteous; we have also been raised to new life in Christ. We are a new creation. And this new reality should encourage and motivate us to "be who we are" and to "become what we are" in Christ.

Chapter Nine

FUTURE RESURRECTION

And we'll drink and dance
with one hand free
and have the world so easily.
And, oh, we'll be a sight to see
back in the high life again.

STEVE WINWOOD

EVERYONE HAS LIKELY HAD THE EXPERIENCE of looking forward to a future event—an exciting trip, a move to a new location, summer vacation, a sixteenth birthday, going to college, a wedding day, or the birth of a child. We often become enamored with the thought of such events and experience great longing and anticipation. This is the way we should be with our future redemption, inheritance, and salvation in Christ. The future for believers is so wonderful and amazing that we should be in awe of the eternity that awaits us. Of course, God doesn't want us to lose our sense of the present, the joy that we can experience in this life, and the call that God gives us before Jesus' second coming. But God reveals certain things about the future to give us hope and motivation in the present.

One of my favorite songs is "Back in the High Life Again" by Steve Winwood because it provides a picture of the way life can be at times, a picture of life as it was meant to be. God created a good world. He looked at his creation and said it was "very good" (see Gen 1:31). But the fall introduced sin, evil, a severed relationship with God, strained human relationships, depression, war, suffering, sadness, toil, disease, disappointment, and death.

The hope of redemption is that all of this will be done away with and replaced by a restored relationship with God, restored human relationships, righteousness, peace, victory, healing, hope, and resurrection life. One of the amazing and exciting things is that we get glimpses of that future life here and now. An intimate time of worship, a wonderfully fulfilling day of work, a sweet time of fellowship with friends, an enjoyable experience of recreation, or a cherished conversation with a close friend. These are little previews of the life to come, life as it was meant to be. The eternity that God has in store for his children is wondrous indeed, and this wonderful eternity is the topic of this chapter.

As we have seen, there is an "already/not yet" character to salvation. In the previous chapter, our focus was on what God has already accomplished for believers in Christ. In this chapter, our focus is on the "not yet" or the future character of salvation in Christ. What God began with his first promise of redemption in Genesis 3:15, he is still at work to complete. Only in the future (when Jesus returns) will this work of salvation reach its consummation. The great hope for Christians is what is still to come. In this chapter, we will continue to trace the same redemptive themes, but the focus will be on their future fulfillment. For the believer, there are still future hopes and promises for a restored relationship with God, dwelling in God's presence, and reigning with God. Consequently, there are also future resurrection hopes. As in the other chapters, my discussion will be centered on the hope and promise of resurrection, but I will demonstrate how these resurrection hopes are tied to the other redemptive themes.

The theological term for the future hope of believers is *glorification*. The term is most often used to refer to the final and eternal state of believers in the new creation, and this will be the primary topic of discussion in this chapter. But we will first consider another future event that precedes final glorification for believers: the intermediate state. The intermediate state refers to the plight of believers after they die, but before Jesus' second coming.

THE INTERMEDIATE STATE

Many Christians in our modern culture believe that going to heaven after death represents the final piece of the puzzle—the consummation of salvation. To be sure, going to heaven after death is a very important piece of the puzzle, but according to the Bible it is not the final piece. In light of this, Bible scholars have often referred to it as the intermediate state, as opposed to the eternal state after Jesus' second coming. Reflecting on the fulfillment of God's redemptive purposes clarifies what is true and not true of the intermediate state.[1]

First, Scripture communicates that believers go to be with the Lord when they die. Jesus says to the thief on the cross, "Truly I tell you, today you will be with me in paradise" (Lk 23:43). The term *paradise* in Scripture refers to the dwelling place of God.[2] With this short statement Jesus reveals much about the intermediate state: after death believers are with Jesus and in the dwelling place of God. In Philippians, as a result of his imprisonment, Paul contemplates the possibility of two outcomes: death or deliverance from death with future fruitful ministry. Paul's desire is that, "whether by life or by death," Christ would be exalted (Phil 1:20). Although Paul desires to depart and be with Christ (Phil 1:23), he is convinced that he will continue to live and to minister (Phil 1:24-26). For our purposes, it is important to recognize that to "depart" (i.e., to die) is to be with Christ.

In one of his visions in Revelation, John sees the souls of martyred saints "under the altar" (Rev 6:9). The phrase "under the altar" is reminiscent of Old Testament temple imagery and communicates that the martyred saints are in God's presence and are protected by God. Similarly, in Revelation 7:9-17 a great multitude from every nation, tribe, people, and language clothed in white robes are "standing before the throne and before the Lamb" (Rev 7:9). This great multitude represents God's people "who have come out of the great tribulation" (Rev 7:14) and who are now in God's presence. These people are before God's throne, serve the Lord in his

---

[1]For discussions of the intermediate state, see John M. Frame, *Systematic Theology: An Introduction to Christian Belief* (Phillipsburg, NJ: P&R, 2013), 1075-78; Robert L. Reymond, *A New Systematic Theology of the Christian Faith* (Nashville: Thomas Nelson, 1998), 1017-18; Louis Berkhof, *Systematic Theology*, new combined ed. (Grand Rapids, MI: Eerdmans, 1996), 679-94.

[2]In addition to Lk 23:43, see also 2 Cor 12:4 and Rev 2:7.

heavenly temple, and are protected and comforted by God (Rev 7:14-17). While some understand "the great tribulation" as a future event from which earthly believers are rescued, the natural reading is that "the great tribulation" refers to the time of suffering and testing in this life.[3] Believers who have died in the Lord have been delivered from this time of testing and tribulation and are now in God's presence. The consistent testimony of Scripture is that believers go to be with the Lord after they die. This experience of being in God's presence is an experience of life after death. It is not the final resurrection, but believers nonetheless experience life in God's presence in the intermediate state.

Second, those who are with the Lord in heaven experience a greater restoration in their relationship with the Lord. Although not explicitly stated, the implication of Scripture is that believers are set free from the presence of sin when they die and go to be with the Lord. The consistent testimony of Scripture is that sinful humanity cannot dwell in God's presence without God's provision for sin. For those who have come out of the great tribulation, the only necessary and efficacious provision is the sacrificial work of Jesus. Because "they have washed their robes and made them white in the blood of the Lamb" (Rev 7:14), they are forgiven and able to enter God's presence. The description that they serve the Lord "day and night in his temple" (Rev 7:15) implies that they are set free from the presence of sin. In this restored relationship, those who have gone to be with the Lord will never again hunger or thirst, are set free from the suffering of this life, and will have every tear from their eyes wiped away by God (Rev 7:16-17).

In addition to dwelling in God's presence and being set free from the presence of sin, believers in the intermediate state reign with God and are participants of "the first resurrection" (Rev 20:5). This brings us to the third and fourth themes we have traced—reigning with God and resurrection. Although the interpretation of Revelation 20:4-6 is debated, in my view this

---

[3]Thus, "the great tribulation" refers to the entire time period between Jesus' first and second coming. See also Revelation 1:9, where the same Greek word for tribulation in Revelation 7:14 is translated as "suffering." In Revelation 1:9, the reference is clearly to the present time period between the first and second coming of Christ.

passage describes the experience of believers in the intermediate state.[4] In the description of his vision, John writes,

> I saw thrones on which were seated those who had been given authority to judge. And I saw the souls of those who had been beheaded because of their testimony about Jesus and because of the word of God. They had not worshiped the beast or its image and had not received its mark on their foreheads or their hands. They came to life and reigned with Christ a thousand years. (The rest of the dead did not come to life until the thousand years were ended.) This is the first resurrection. Blessed and holy are those who share in the first resurrection. The second death has no power over them, but they will be priests of God and of Christ and will reign with him for a thousand years. (Rev 20:4-6)

Similar to Revelation 6:9, this passage serves as a source of encouragement for believers who face persecution. What happens to believers when they die? What happens to believers when they are killed for their faith?[5] They come to life and reign with Christ! So believers who die in the Lord have a wonderful future ahead of them, even their immediate future.

The references to "the first resurrection" and "the second death" (Rev 20:5-6) imply a "second resurrection" and a "first death." The first death is the death that all people experience, and the first resurrection likely refers to the experience of believers who are with the Lord after the first death. Those who die in the Lord immediately experience a resurrection of sorts since they come to life and dwell with the Lord after death. In depicting this "first resurrection," John writes that he saw "souls" that "came to life" (Rev 20:4). The "souls" that come to life are in God's presence and participate in Christ's heavenly reign. In describing this first resurrection, Beale writes, "It is reasonable to interpret the ascent of the soul at the time of death into the Lord's presence as a form of spiritual resurrection."[6] Since believers take part in the first resurrection,

---

[4] I understand Rev 20:1-6 and the millennium as the time period between the first and second coming of Jesus. For an introduction to and discussion of this view, see Anthony A. Hoekema, "Amillennialism," in *The Meaning of the Millennium: Four Views*, ed. Robert G. Clouse (Downers Grove, IL: IVP Academic, 1977), 155-87.

[5] Although it is the martyred saints who are singled out as coming to life and reigning with Christ (Rev 20:4), this reality is true for all believers who die in the Lord.

[6] G. K. Beale with David H. Campbell, *Revelation: A Shorter Commentary* (Grand Rapids, MI: Eerdmans, 2015), 443; see 433-51 for a thorough discussion and defense of this interpretation.

they are assured that the second death, eternal punishment of unbelievers, has no power over them.

The implied second resurrection is no doubt a reference to the final and still future bodily resurrection of believers when Jesus returns. Not only do believers come to life after death; they also reign with Christ (for a thousand years) (Rev 20:4). In line with this interpretation of Revelation 20, the "thousand years" is a symbolic number that refers to the entire time period between the first and second coming of Christ. After death and before Jesus' second coming, believers come to life and reign with Christ in heaven. This reality and experience highlights another connection between resurrection and reigning with God.

Believers who die in the Lord have been set free from the presence of sin, are in God's presence, reign with Christ, and take part in the first resurrection. In his letter to the Philippians, Paul writes that "to die is gain" (Phil 1:21). In comparison to this present earthly life, the reality of departing and being with Christ is "better by far" (Phil 1:23). In addition to the redemptive realities discussed above, John Piper details five blessings that come to believers at death: (1) their spirits will be perfected, (2) they will be set free from pain and suffering, (3) their souls will experience rest, (4) they will feel at home, and (5) they will be in the presence of the Lord.[7]

Although the intermediate step represents a significant step in redemption, it is not the consummation of God's plan. When God breathes life into Adam (Gen 2:7), there is a profound unity between the body and soul. God's purpose for Adam and all his descendants is a physical and embodied life in God's creation. Thus, God's original purpose for humanity is not a disembodied soul, even if the soul is in the presence of the Lord. In Revelation 6:10, the martyred saints in God's presence cry out, "How long, Sovereign Lord, holy and true, until you judge the inhabitants of the earth and avenge our blood?" God's answer is that they must wait a little longer until the full number of the martyrs is reached (Rev 6:11). The saints in heaven are not fully satisfied. Although they are with the Lord and experience relief from sin and the troubles of this life, they still look forward to the consummation of their salvation.

---

[7]John Piper, "It Is Great Gain to Die: Five Reasons Why," in *A Godward Life* (Sisters, OR: Multnomah, 1997), 50-52.

Specifically, those who are with the Lord in heaven look forward to God's future judgment (see again Rev 6:10), their future bodily resurrection (Rom 8:23-25), and the new creation (Rom 8:20-22).

Table 9.1. The intermediate state

REDEMPTIVE THEME	FULFILLMENT
Restored relationship with God	Free from the presence of sin
God's presence	Experience life and serve in God's presence
Serving as God's vice-regents	Reign with Christ in heaven
Life and resurrection	Partakers of the first resurrection; life with God in heaven

THE ETERNAL STATE

God's plan of redemption is a long process full of twists and turns and various fulfillments. But God's promise to bring victory for his people in Genesis 3:15 has always moved toward the hope of a restored relationship with God, life in God's presence, reigning with God, and life after death. These redemptive themes find their final fulfillment with the second coming of Jesus and in the new creation. In this section, I will discuss the final fulfillment of these redemptive themes and explain how they are closely tied to the hope of resurrection.

Relationship with God. Through faith in Christ, believers have already been reconciled with God, justified before God, adopted as his children, born again, and created anew. Moreover, believers will be set free from the presence of sin when they go to be with the Lord after death. So the question is, What lies in the future for believers in the restoration of their relationship with God?

In the new creation, believers will experience the final and complete fulfillment of the new-covenant promises and realities.[8] In Jeremiah 31:31-34 God declares that he will bring about a new covenant that will be different from the old covenant. Because God's law will be completely written on the hearts and minds of his people (Jer 31:33), they will no longer sin but rather

---

[8]In addition to Jer 31:31-34, see Ezek 11:17-21; 37:23.

be perfectly faithful to God.[9] God's promise that he "will be their God, / and they will be [his] people" (Jer 31:33) will reach its final fulfillment. In the context of Jeremiah 30–33, these new-covenant hopes, promises, and prophecies are closely connected to the restoration hopes and promises for Israel. Thus, the fulfillment of Jeremiah 31:31-34 is tied to the consummate hopes of life in the land, a fulfillment that is realized only in resurrection life in the new creation. So even though believers are free from the presence of sin in the intermediate state, they do not experience the final fulfillment of the new-covenant promises and realities until Jesus' second coming and the onset of the new creation.

In addition to the final fulfillment of the new-covenant promises, believers will be openly vindicated before all of creation at the final judgment and in the new creation. The resurrection of Jesus served as vindication that he was the Messiah and that he was righteous. Jesus was vindicated by God and before God. But there is also a sense in which Jesus' resurrection served as his vindication before others. Specifically, his resurrection served as his open and public vindication (at least to those to whom he appeared) that he is the Messiah and God's righteous servant. Those who are united to Christ have already been justified. They are forgiven of sin and declared righteous before God. However, their justification is only before God and thus in secret.

But consider what Paul writes in Romans 8:19: "For the creation waits in eager expectation for the children of God to be revealed." At the final judgment and in the new creation, the vindication of God's children will be open and public for all to see. In this same context, Paul writes of the "glory that will be revealed in us" (Rom 8:18) and that "we wait eagerly for our adoption to sonship, the redemption of our bodies" (Rom 8:23). Significantly, this future open vindication of believers is explicitly connected to resurrection.[10] As Beale writes, "Their physical resurrection will be undeniable proof of the validity of their faith, which had already declared

---

[9]Since nothing impure will ever enter the new Jerusalem (Rev 21:27), it is clear that believers will be set free from the presence of sin in the new creation.

[10]G. K. Beale also notes the connection between resurrection and future justification; see his discussions in *A New Testament Biblical Theology: The Unfolding of the Old Testament in the New* (Grand Rapids, MI: Baker Academic, 2011), 497-526, 902-4. See also the Westminster Shorter Catechism (Question 38) which reads, "At the resurrection, believers being raised up in glory, shall

them righteous in their past life."[11] Once again, a right relationship with God is closely tied to resurrection. In their present experience, believers are already justified "by faith," but at the final judgment, believers will be justified "by sight" through their bodily resurrection.[12] Consequently, the final pieces of the puzzle in a restored relationship with God—the final fulfillment of Jeremiah 31:31-34 and open vindication—only come into focus when Jesus returns and are inseparably linked with resurrection hopes.

God's life-giving presence. In redemptive history God has dwelled with his people in various ways—in the Garden of Eden, by leading his people with smoke and fire, in the tabernacle, in the temple, in the person of Jesus, and through the indwelling of the Holy Spirit. In the new creation there will be no physical temple "because the Lord God Almighty and the Lamb are its temple" (Rev 21:22). The entire new creation will be the temple and the dwelling place of God because all of creation will be permeated by God's presence. In fulfillment of Habakkuk's prophecy, "the earth will be filled with the knowledge of the glory of the LORD / as the waters cover the sea" (Hab 2:14). God's promise that he will place his sanctuary among his people and that his dwelling place will be with his people (Ezek 37:26-28) will have reached its fulfillment. In Revelation 21:3 we read, "Look! God's dwelling place is now among the people, and he will dwell with them. They will be his people, and God himself will be with them and be their God."

This new creation represents the fulfillment of Genesis 1:28 and God's purpose to extend his reign and his dwelling place throughout the earth. God's commission to Adam and Eve was to make the entire earth his garden, but as humanity populated and filled the earth, this temple-garden would inevitably grow into a city, now realized in the new Jerusalem that comes down from heaven (Rev 21:1-2). In contrast to the original garden, nothing impure will ever enter the new Jerusalem (Rev 21:27). It will be God's sanctuary and the place where he dwells with his people forever.

---

be openly acknowledged and acquitted in the day of judgment, and made perfectly blessed in the full enjoying of God, to all eternity."

[11]Beale, *New Testament Biblical Theology*, 498.

[12]Richard B. Gaffin Jr., *By Faith, Not by Sight: Paul and the Order of Salvation*, 2nd ed. (Phillipsburg, NJ: P&R, 2013), 101.

In the new heaven and new earth, God's life-giving presence will pervade the new creation. This new creation is the only place that is suitable for the new resurrection life of God's people. As a result of Adam's sin, in addition to all of humanity being subject to the effects of the fall and death, creation also was subject to decay and death. In his plan of redemption God is committed to providing not only resurrection life for his people but also a new creation that is no longer subject to frustration and in bondage to decay (Rom 8:19-21).

In this new creation the throne of God and the Lamb are in the middle of the city (Rev 22:1-2). From this throne the river of the water of life flows through the middle of the city, and the tree of life stands on each side of the river (Rev 22:2-3). The river of the water of life that flows from the throne of God and the Lamb is reminiscent of Eden (Gen 2:10) and signifies God's life-giving presence that pervades the new creation. Moreover, just as the tree of life was available to Adam and Eve at creation, the tree of life in the new creation represents resurrection life for God's people from all the nations of the world (Rev 22:2). The description of the new creation as God's temple reinforces that God's presence is tied to life and resurrection. The future hope of believers is explicitly tied to the new creation as the source of God's life-giving presence. This is the place where believers will experience the fullness of resurrection life.

Reigning with God. With the second coming of Jesus, God's purpose for his kingship to extend to the ends of the earth will be realized. Indeed, the return of Jesus means that

> the kingdom of the world has become
>> the kingdom of our Lord and of his Messiah,
>> and he will reign for ever and ever. (Rev 11:15)

As we have seen, God's intention for humanity through all Scripture—from creation to the consummation of redemption—is to serve as his vice-regents. Through faith in Jesus, believers are enabled to join and participate in Jesus' eschatological and eternal kingdom. This kingdom has been inaugurated with Jesus' first coming but will not be consummated until his second coming. While believers are already a part of this kingdom and already reign with Christ, they nevertheless look forward to the day when this kingdom and their reign with Christ will be consummated. This future hope will be realized in the new creation when believers "will reign for ever and ever" (Rev 22:5).

As in all aspects of redemption, reigning with God is intimately connected with union with Christ. In Revelation 3:21 Jesus promises, "To the one who is victorious, I will give the right to sit with me on my throne, just as I was victorious and sat down with my Father on his throne." This promise brings into focus that believers' victory and reign with Christ is tied to Jesus' victory and reign. Although the text does not clarify what is meant by "victorious," Jesus' resurrection from the dead is likely in view. Jesus' promise in Revelation 2:7 makes the connection more explicit: "To the one who is victorious, I will give the right to eat from the tree of life, which is in the paradise of God." The tree of life is a clear motif for creation life before the fall and for resurrection life in the new creation. Both Revelation 3:21 and Revelation 2:7 speak of the promise of future victory for believers, one promise clearly connected to reigning with Christ and the other clearly connected to resurrection.

In his first letter to the Corinthians, Paul also emphasizes that reigning with God in the consummated sense (1 Cor 4:8) and bodily resurrection (1 Cor 15:22-24) are both future events. In a similar vein, Paul writes,

> If we died with him,
>> we will also live with him;
> if we endure,
>> we will also reign with him. (2 Tim 2:11-12)

Here Paul explicitly connects future resurrection hopes with reigning with God in the future. In all these passages, the hope for those who trust in Christ and persevere in faith is resurrection and reigning with God in the future. And, of course, this demonstrates again that these redemptive hopes are inseparably linked. Scripture thus emphasizes that believers must experience resurrection to reign with God.

Table 9.2. Glorification / eternal state / new creation

REDEMPTIVE THEME	FULFILLMENT
Restored relationship with God	Open vindication; fulfillment of new-covenant promises
Life in God's presence	New creation as the temple; dwell with God forever; tree of life
Serving as God's vice-regents	Reign with Christ forever in the new creation
Life and resurrection	Glorified bodily resurrection

Future bodily resurrection. In the new creation, believers will experience the final fulfillment of a restored relationship with God, God's life-giving presence, and reigning with God. It should not come as a surprise, then, that believers will also experience the final fulfillment of resurrection when Jesus returns and in the new creation.[13] In Philippians 3:20-21 Paul writes about this hope and emphasizes its connection with Jesus' second coming: "But our citizenship is in heaven. And we eagerly await a Savior from there, the Lord Jesus Christ, who, by the power that enables him to bring everything under his control, will transform our lowly bodies so that they will be like his glorious body." Whereas death entered the picture with Adam's sin, the second Adam brings resurrection through his life, death, and resurrection.[14] Moreover, the future resurrection bodies of believers will be like Christ's resurrection body. Whereas their present bodies are "lowly," God will transform them to be like the "glorious" resurrected body of Jesus (Phil 3:20-21).

As Philippians 3:20-21 clarifies, Jesus' resurrection body provides the paradigm for believers' resurrection bodies. To some degree, we can only

---

[13]As stated in the introduction, my purpose in this book is a biblical theology of resurrection, and my focus is on the resurrection of God's people. But in addition to the future resurrection of believers, Scripture teaches the future resurrection of unbelievers. Daniel prophesies that some will be raised to everlasting life and that others will rise to shame and everlasting contempt (Dan 12:1-2). Jesus emphasizes that all of the dead will hear his voice, and believers will rise to life and unbelievers to condemnation (Jn 5:28-29). Paul proclaims that there will be a resurrection of the righteous and the wicked (Acts 24:15). Since they are not in a right relationship with God, unbelievers will be raised to condemnation and judgment (Jn 5:28-29), and they will be punished with everlasting destruction and shut out from God's presence and glory (2 Thess 1:8-9). Rather than experiencing God's glorious presence, unbelievers will suffer eternal judgment and punishment in God's presence (Rev 14:9-11).

[14]See again 1 Cor 15:21.

speculate on the specific similarities and differences. In their descriptions of Jesus' resurrection, the gospel accounts clarify that there will be continuity between our present lowly bodies and future glorified bodies. Moreover, Jesus emphasizes that his resurrection body is a physical body with flesh and bones, and invites his disciples to touch him (Lk 24:39). He even invites them to a meal and eats a piece of fish in their presence (Lk 24:41-43).[15]

Although people are at times kept from recognizing Jesus (Lk 24:16) or slow to recognize him because of their confusion, surprise, or amazement (Lk 24:41; Jn 20:13), the disciples are in general able to recognize Jesus because of the continuity between his previous body and his present resurrection body. Moreover, Jesus shows his hands and his feet to his disciples (Lk 24:39-40), presumably to highlight the marks and scars where the nails were placed. When he later appears to Thomas (who made it clear that he would not believe that Jesus was raised from the dead unless he personally saw and touched his hands and side), he invites him to touch his hands, where the nails were, and his side, where he was pierced by the sword (Jn 20:24-29).

Although there will be continuity between believers' present and future bodies, Scripture also makes it clear there will be some important differences. In the case of Jesus, it is impossible to discern whether his ability suddenly to appear or disappear (Jn 20:19-29; Lk 24:31) is the result of his glorified resurrection body or his divinity. The passage that most clearly elucidates the contrast between believers' present and future bodies is 1 Corinthians 15:35-49. Jesus' resurrection is the basis for the future resurrection of those united to Christ (1 Cor 15:21-23), and his glorified body is the paradigm for the future resurrection bodies of his people (1 Cor 15:35-49). On the one hand, believers' present bodies are perishable, sown in dishonor, sown in weakness, and sown as natural bodies (1 Cor 15:42-44). On the other hand, their future resurrection bodies will be imperishable, raised in glory, raised in power, and raised as spiritual bodies (1 Cor 15:42-44). We will consider each of the contrasts in turn.

The first contrast is between perishable and imperishable. At present, believers' bodies are perishable, meaning they are subject to death. In

---

[15]See also Jn 21:10-13.

1 Corinthians 15:50, when Paul writes that flesh and blood cannot enter the kingdom of God, his point is that present earthly bodies cannot enter the kingdom because they are stained by sin and subject to death.[16] Since the new creation will be characterized by life and resurrection, believers must have new resurrection bodies to inherit this new creation. Since their future resurrection bodies will be imperishable, they will not be subject to death.

The second contrast is between dishonor and glory. This terminology suggests that believers' future resurrection bodies represent an indispensable part of their future glorification. Whereas sin and the fall brought shame and dishonor to humanity, so much so that Adam and Eve attempted to hide their shame (Gen 2:25; 3:7), believers' future resurrection bodies will restore them to their rightful dignity as redeemed images of God who reflect God's glory as he intended.

Third, whereas believers' present bodies are weak because of sin and the fall, their future glorified bodies will be raised in power. Although our earthly experiences are not all the same, all people understand well how the bumps, bruises, pains, injuries, illnesses, disabilities, and aging associated with this life demonstrate the weakness of our present bodies. By way of contrast, believers' future resurrection bodies will be raised in power, no more subject to handicap, weakness, injury, or aging.

In his song "The Runner," Alex MacDonald tells the story of his brother, who earlier in his life was a great runner. On account of serving as a surgeon in India, MacDonald's brother developed multiple sclerosis, which led to him no longer being able to run.[17] While this is undoubtedly an earthly tragedy, MacDonald recounts this story and sings of his brother's glorious future:

> You ran to the poor man who had the bite of death
> The kiss of life for him, the kiss of death for you
> You ran the second mile for him, you gave him your own breath
> Now the legs that ran for others will no longer run for you

---

[16] As discussed in chapter one, Paul's quotation of Gen 2:7 in 1 Cor 15:45 perhaps implies that Adam, Eve, and all humanity descended from them would have needed new bodies even if they had not fallen in sin.

[17] For the background story of "The Runner," see www.alexjmacdonald.co.uk/information.htm.

You can't run in the fields and you can't run in the woods
On the track and on the hill your running days are done
But you'll run in the city where the river flows
You'll fly on the mountain when the day comes.[18]

In the new creation, he will run again! If this life is all there is, then Christians who give themselves in service to the gospel, and perhaps suffer trial, tribulation, or death as a result, "are of all people most to be pitied" (1 Cor 15:19). But the glorious hope of resurrection means that believers' bodies will no longer be marked by weakness. They will be raised in power. And those who cannot run and jump in this life will run and jump in the life to come. As the prophet Isaiah promises, "the eyes of the blind [will] be opened," "the ears of the deaf [will be] unstopped," "the lame [will] leap like a deer," and "the mute tongue [will] shout for joy" (Is 35:5-6). The resurrection is good news indeed!

The final contrast is between present natural bodies and future spiritual bodies. Within the context of 1 Corinthians and Pauline theology, it is essential to understand "spiritual" as a reference to the Holy Spirit. In Romans 8:11 Paul writes, "And if the Spirit of him who raised Jesus from the dead is living in you, he who raised Christ from the dead will also give life to your mortal bodies because of his Spirit who lives in you." Just as the Spirit was integral to creation life and to Jesus' resurrection, the Spirit will animate the bodies of God's people for their final and future resurrection. The contrast between the natural body and the body animated by the Spirit corresponds to the contrast between the first man (Adam), who was "of the dust of the earth," and the second man (Jesus), who is "of heaven" (1 Cor 15:44-47). As a result, the contrast is not between the physical and the immaterial, but rather "between *corruptible physicality*, on the one hand, and *incorruptible physicality*, on the other."[19] Jesus' bodily resurrection is the paradigm for those who are united to him, and those who "have borne the image of the earthly man" will also "bear the image of the heavenly man" (1 Cor 15:49).[20]

---

[18]Alex J. MacDonald, "The Runner," www.alexjmacdonald.co.uk/CD%20Lyrics.pdf, ©Alex J. MacDonald, 2008. Used with permission.

[19]N. T. Wright, *Surprised by Hope: Rethinking Heaven, the Resurrection, and the Mission of the Church* (New York: HarperOne, 2008), 156. Emphasis original.

[20]The context of 1 Cor 15:35-49—namely, the emphasis on future fulfillment—leads me to prefer the future indicative ("we will") textual variant in 1 Cor 15:49 over the subjunctive ("let us").

Essential to a biblical understanding of future resurrection is that a "transformation" must take place (1 Cor 15:51). Since flesh and blood cannot enter the kingdom of God (1 Cor 15:50), all believers, both those who have passed away and those who are alive when Christ returns, must be "changed." As Paul makes clear, the reason for this transformation is that "the perishable must clothe itself with the imperishable, and the mortal with immortality" (1 Cor 15:53). Paul emphasizes that this transformation is an eschatological, glorified, and physical transformation. It is not merely a return to the pre-fall state of Adam, since the body of the first Adam, even before the fall, is contrasted with the glorified and eschatological body of the last Adam (1 Cor 15:45-49).

The first man was "of the dust of the earth" (1 Cor 15:47) and "the earthly man" (1 Cor 15:48-49), while the second man is "of heaven" (1 Cor 15:47) and "the heavenly man" (1 Cor 15:48).[21] And this contrast is not between physical and immaterial but rather between the original body of Adam, subject to sin and death, and the present glorified body of Christ, identified with the Spirit and empowered by God.[22] Only this transformed, glorified, imperishable, immortal, and Spirit-animated resurrection body is fit to dwell with God in the glorified new creation. For believers, the good news is that the experience of resurrection life in the new creation will be even greater than Adam's Edenic pre-fall experience of life.[23]

In addition to his description of the future resurrection body, Paul reveals when this future resurrection will take place. At Christ's second coming, believers who are on the earth will be transformed into their resurrection bodies, and the dead in Christ will be raised imperishable (1 Cor 15:50-53; 1 Thess 4:13-17). Amid concerns over what will happen to believers who have died, Paul communicates that the dead in Christ will not be disadvantaged

---

[21]In 2 Cor 5:1-5 Paul also describes the future resurrection as "a building from God, an eternal house in heaven," and as being clothed "with our heavenly dwelling." To be raised to life is to be clothed with our heavenly dwelling.

[22]See Herman Ridderbos, *Paul: An Outline of His Theology*, trans. John Richard de Witt (Grand Rapids, MI: Eerdmans, 1975), 540-48.

[23]G. K. Beale and Benjamin L. Gladd note that this notion of "transformation" in resurrection is not elucidated in the Old Testament. Having now been revealed in the New Testament, this transformation is part of the "mystery" of Christ (1 Cor 15:51). See *Hidden but Now Revealed: A Biblical Theology of Mystery* (Downers Grove, IL: IVP Academic, 2014), 129-36.

(1 Thess 4:13-17). Rather, at Jesus' return the dead in Christ will rise first, and believers on the earth will subsequently be caught up with them to meet the Lord in the air (1 Thess 4:16-17). With the second coming of Jesus, the resurrection of believers, and the new creation, God's redemptive plan has reached its culmination. Death, as the great enemy of humanity, will be finally and forever defeated, and believers can say,

> "Death has been swallowed up in victory."
>   "Where, O death, is your victory?
>   Where, O death, is your sting?"

> The sting of death is sin, and the power of sin is the law. But thanks be to God! He gives us the victory through our Lord Jesus Christ. (1 Cor 15:54-57)

CONCLUSION AND APPLICATION

The future inheritance of believers is of utmost importance. God has been faithful to his promises throughout all of history. This gives us confidence that he will keep his promises for the future. There are great promises for believers in the intermediate state. Those who die in the Lord go to be with the Lord, are set free from the presence of sin and the trials of life, reign with the Lord, and are raised from death to life in the first resurrection. Paul describes this experience of being with Christ as "better by far" (Phil 1:23), yet Paul and the other New Testament writers make it clear that this is not the final, ultimate, and eternal experience of redemption.

The full inheritance for believers is fulfilled only with the second coming of Jesus, the final judgment, and the new creation. First, in the final judgment, believers will be openly vindicated before all creation as righteous and as God's children (Rom 8:19). Moreover, they will be fully animated by the Spirit and will experience the consummate fulfillment of the new-covenant promises in the new creation. God's word and law will be written on their hearts and minds, and they will be completely faithful to God's covenant. Second, since the new creation represents the final temple, believers will dwell forever in God's presence. Moreover, their access to the tree of life emphasizes the close relationship between God's presence and resurrection life. Third, in the new creation, believers will reign with Christ forever. While life in the kingdom is presently still characterized by sin, suffering, and death, believers in the new creation will reign with Christ in righteousness, victory, and life.

Finally, God's redemptive plan includes the glorified bodily resurrection of believers. With their bodily resurrection, believers will rejoice that sin and death have been defeated, and they will reign forever in their resurrected bodies in the new creation. With the final resurrection, we should not miss two things of central importance. First, resurrection is organically and closely linked with salvation throughout all of redemptive history. Second, the bodily resurrection of believers and the new creation represent the final pieces of the redemptive puzzle. Without the final resurrection, God's redemptive plan is not complete, and the sting of sin and the penalty of death are not taken away. But with the bodily resurrection and the new creation, God's redemptive plan is brought to fruition.

The future resurrection of believers is an exciting and important doctrine. Not only will the sting of sin in death be done away with; the repercussions of a fallen creation and sin's effects on physical life will also be amended. In fulfillment of Isaiah 35:6 and Jesus' miracles, the lame will leap like a deer. Moreover, we will experience the consummate fulfillment of physical life in God's new and perfect creation. N. T. Wright explains,

> Why will we be given new bodies? According to the early Christians, the purpose of this new body will be to rule wisely over God's new world. Forget those images about lounging around playing harps. There will be work to do and we shall relish doing it. All the skills and talents we have put to God's service in this present life—and perhaps too the interests and likings we gave up because they conflicted with our vocation—will be enhanced and ennobled and given back to us to be exercised to his glory.[24]

We will reign over creation as God intended. This means God-glorifying and soul-satisfying labor, the kind of labor God intended for us at creation before the curse of the fall. Recreation will be a part of the new creation, the perfect fulfillment of God-glorifying and edifying physical activity and leisure. Relationships will be restored to perfect unity. This includes our relationship with the Lord and with others. The wonderful friendships and conversations

---

[24]Wright, *Surprised by Hope*, 161.

that we experience in this life are only foretastes of the relational glories to come.

According to Scripture, we will also eat in the new creation. The foretastes of the Passover meal and the Lord's Supper will be fulfilled in the wedding feast of the lamb (Rev 19:7-9). We will dine with Jesus! Consider the significance of this. In this life, we dine with family and friends. And the fact that we will dine with Jesus means that we are his family and friends.[25] And let's not forget that we will dance. The Old Testament prophets proclaim that God's people will go out to dance with the joyful (Jer 31:4), that men and women will dance and be glad (Jer 31:13), and that God will turn mourning into gladness, and sorrow into comfort and joy (Jer 31:13). This is an eternity that we can be excited about and look forward to! Without the bodily resurrection, we cannot experience the life God intended for us in creation and the life that he brings to us with the consummation of the new creation.

---

[25]See the discussion in Frame, *Systematic Theology*, 1067-69.

Chapter Ten

CONCLUDING THOUGHTS ON RESURRECTION LIFE

It is well with my soul.

HORATIO SPAFFORD

WHAT I HOPE has become clear in this book is that life and resurrection are major themes in Scripture. The hope of eternal life is so central to the story of the Bible that it was promised by God even before the beginning of time (Titus 1:1-3). Not only is resurrection life a major theme in Scripture; it is inseparably linked with other major themes and redemptive realities. God's program for bringing about resurrection life is a long process with many twists and turns and ups and downs. In the old covenant, God gives promises, prophecies, and pictures of resurrection life. But with the first coming of Jesus, the new age breaks into the old age, and the age of resurrection begins. Jesus has been raised from the dead and those who are united to Christ have already been raised up spiritually and have already crossed over from death to life, yet believers still look forward to the consummation of their salvation and the consummation of resurrection life. In concluding this book, I will discuss two ways that the hope of resurrection should shape our Christian lives. First, future resurrection is an indispensable part of God's redemptive plan and therefore represents a primary goal for Christians. Second, believers are called to live in light of resurrection hopes.

RESURRECTION AS THE GOAL OF THE CHRISTIAN LIFE

When Paul recounts his previous life in Judaism, he reflects on his various credentials but maintains that whatever "gains" he had in the past, he now considers as nothing for the sake of Christ (Phil 3:4-7). Although he considered himself "faultless" by the standards of Jewish law, he considers all of that a "loss" compared to knowing Jesus, being found in Jesus, and having a righteousness that is not from himself or his own work but rather is received through faith in Christ (Phil 3:6-9). As Paul reflects on this, he writes, "I want to know Christ—yes, to know the power of his resurrection and participation in his sufferings, becoming like him in his death, and so, somehow, attaining to the resurrection from the dead" (Phil 3:10-11).[1] Paul's hope, goal, and motivation for the Christian life is resurrection from the dead.

To attain resurrection, Paul is willing to consider his past and indeed all his accomplishments as "loss," and he is willing even to identify with Christ in his sufferings and death. For those who are united to Christ, Christ's death becomes their death, and Christ's resurrection is the basis for their resurrection. In Philippians 3 and in many other places in Scripture, the path for followers of Jesus is to share in Jesus' sufferings in the present, but to share in Jesus' glory in the future.[2]

For Paul, the hope and the goal of resurrection far outweigh the cost of identifying with Christ in his sufferings. Paul makes it clear that he has not obtained or arrived at his goal yet, but he presses on toward the goal for which Christ Jesus took hold of him (Phil 3:12). Paul's focus is "forgetting what is behind and straining toward what is ahead" and "[pressing] on toward the goal to win the prize for which God has called me heavenward in Christ Jesus" (Phil 3:13-14). The goal that Paul has in mind here undoubtedly is

---

[1] In this passage Paul's seamless movement between justification and the hope of resurrection emphasizes again the close relationship between these two redemptive realities.

[2] In addition to Phil 3:7-14, see Phil 2:1-11 and Mk 8:34-38. Here I do not mean that believers' suffering is identical to Jesus' suffering or that believers' suffering atones for sin, nor do I mean that believers' glory will be identical to Christ's glory.

resurrection. This is confirmed when he connects believers' citizenship in heaven with Christ's return and the future bodily resurrection of believers a few verses later (Phil 3:20-21). This passage reveals that resurrection is a primary goal for the Christian. The hope of resurrection is not subsidiary or inconsequential in the Christian life.[3] Resurrection life is at the very heart of God's redemptive plan.

Paul's outlook and the biblical doctrine of resurrection should challenge and shape our thinking. Our ultimate hope is that the sting of death will be conquered (1 Cor 15:56), that death will be swallowed up in victory (1 Cor 15:54), and that we will be raised from the dead—that Jesus "will transform our lowly bodies so that they will be like his glorious body" (Phil 3:21). So many times, Christians limit their hopes for eternal life to something akin to a heavenly spiritual experience in God's presence. A restored relationship with God and dwelling in God's presence are essential in God's redemptive plan, but we must also remember that God created us for life and created us to serve as his vice-regents in reigning over creation. Redemption is not complete until God's life-giving purposes have been fulfilled in the bodily resurrection of his people. In their resurrection, God's people will serve him in the fullness of the new covenant, experience the fullness of God's presence in the new creation, and reign with God forever.

RESURRECTION HOPES AS ENCOURAGEMENT

The resurrection changes everything. In our study of resurrection in the New Testament, we considered three stages of fulfillment for eschatological resurrection: (1) the resurrection of Jesus (chapter seven), (2) the initial spiritual resurrection of believers when they believe in Christ (chapter eight), and (3) the future bodily resurrection of believers at Jesus' second coming (chapter nine).[4] In light of these realities, believers are called to live resurrection lives.

---

[3]See Timothy Keller, *Hope in Times of Fear: The Resurrection and the Meaning of Easter* (New York: Viking, 2021). In this book, Keller explains how the hope of resurrection is life-changing for all areas of life, including relationships, justice, suffering, and the future.

[4]Richard B. Gaffin Jr. identifies these three stages of eschatological fulfillment in *By Faith, Not by Sight: Paul and the Order of Salvation*, 2nd ed. (Phillipsburg, NJ: P&R, 2013), 72. In his book *Lifted: Experiencing the Resurrection Life* (Phillipsburg, NJ: P&R, 2010), Sam Allberry more or less identifies these same three realities in his chapters devoted to assurance because of Jesus' resurrection,

I will highlight three applications that correspond with these stages of eschatological resurrection fulfillment.

Table 10.1. The significance of resurrection in the Christian life

ESCHATOLOGICAL RESURRECTION FULFILLMENT	SIGNIFICANCE FOR THE CHRISTIAN LIFE
The resurrection of Jesus Christ (past)	Basis for resurrection of believers (on account of union with Christ)
Spiritual resurrection of believers through faith in Christ (present reality)	Basis for new life in Christ (resurrection life in the power of the Holy Spirit)
Glorified bodily resurrection of believers at Jesus' second coming (future)	Basis for hope in the midst of trial, tribulation, suffering, and persecution

First, death is not the final word for the believer. Consider these words from Paul in 1 Thessalonians 4:13-14: "Brothers and sisters, we do not want you to be uninformed about those who sleep in death, so that you do not grieve like the rest of mankind, who have no hope. For we believe that Jesus died and rose again, and so we believe that God will bring with Jesus those who have fallen asleep in him." Death is the result of Adam's first sin, and all who sin justly deserve condemnation, punishment, and death. Death is awful. There is no way around it. As the author of Hebrews states, humanity has been kept in slavery because of the fear of death (Heb 2:14-15). But believers have someone who has broken the power of sin, death, and the devil—the Lord Jesus Christ (Heb 2:14-15). Because Jesus rose again, God will also raise up those who have fallen asleep in Jesus (1 Thess 4:13-14).

After the death of his four daughters, Horatio Spafford wrote the song "It Is Well with My Soul" (1873). Consider these lyrics:

> When peace like a river attendeth my way,
> When sorrows like sea billows roll,
> Whatever my lot, Thou hast taught me to say,
> It is well, it is well with my soul.

---

transformation because of the new life that believers have in Christ, and hope because of the future resurrection of believers. Allberry's fourth chapter is devoted to mission—the mission that believers have because of their new life in Christ. This corresponds with my final application point in this book, that because of Jesus' resurrection, believers' labor in the Lord in not in vain (1 Cor 15:58).

. . . .

And Lord, haste the day when my faith shall be sight,
The clouds be rolled back as a scroll;
The trump shall resound, and the Lord shall descend;
Even so, it is well with my soul!

Only the Lord's abiding presence and the hope of future resurrection can sustain us through tragedies and allow us to say, "It is well with my soul." Death is an awful tragedy, but the hope of life after death changes everything. Believers grieve and mourn when they experience the sting, horror, and travesty of death. Jesus himself wept and was even angry at death when his friend Lazarus died. So, we weep, we grieve, and we mourn. But we do not grieve as the rest of humankind. Although we sorely miss our friends and family who have died, death is not the final word for believers. Because of Jesus' resurrection and the future resurrection of his people, we have hope and joy even in the midst of the greatest evil and travesty. This hope is that God will one day raise up believers who have fallen asleep in Jesus.

Second, believers should live resurrection lives because they have already been raised up with Christ spiritually and have been newly created in Christ. In his letters, Paul exhorts his readers to live in light of who they are in Christ. Those who have died with Christ should count themselves dead to sin but alive in Christ Jesus (Rom 6:8-11). Since we have been brought from death to life, we should live in a way that reflects that reality, not letting sin reign in us but offering ourselves to God and living for righteousness rather than wickedness (Rom 6:11-14). In Ephesians 4:22-24 Paul exhorts us "to put off [the] old self" and "to put on the new self, created to be like God in true righteousness and holiness." Whereas our lives were once given to sin, darkness, and death, God now calls and enables us to live for righteousness, light, and life.

Similarly, Peter emphasizes that believers come to Jesus, "the living Stone" (1 Pet 2:4-5). The "Stone" is a reference to Jesus as the messianic cornerstone (1 Pet 2:6-8), and the description of this stone as "living" no doubt highlights Jesus' resurrection. Since they have come to "the living Stone," believers are also "living stones" that are being built into God's house to be a holy priesthood (1 Pet 2:5). The fact that believers have come to the "living" Jesus and are also now "living stones" is the theological foundation for Peter's exhortations in his letter for believers to live out their faith. The teaching of Paul and Peter is clear: since we have been raised to new life in Christ, we are called and enabled to live in light of that new reality.

Third, the hope of future resurrection provides motivation and practical application for believers who live in the time between Jesus' first and second coming. God lets us know about the future in order to encourage us in the present. As a result, we are called to live in light of the hope of future resurrection. Life for all people is a journey through many seasons—times of birth and death, planting and uprooting, killing and healing, tearing down and building, weeping and laughing, and mourning and dancing (Eccles 3:1-4). God reveals some of the wonderful future inheritance for believers to encourage us through trials and difficulties. Peter reminds us that the trials of this life are only "for a little while" (1 Pet 1:6), but believers have an eternal inheritance in Christ (1 Pet 1:3-9). We have received new birth and a living hope because of Jesus' resurrection from the dead (1 Pet 1:3). This eternal inheritance can never perish, spoil, or fade and is kept in heaven and protected by God (1 Pet 1:4-5).

In a similar way, Paul reminds us that Jesus' path to glory was preceded by humility, sacrifice, and service (Phil 2:6-11) in order to encourage believers to live in humility, sacrifice, and service (Phil 2:1-5). It is precisely because of our wonderful future hope and inheritance that we can willingly serve and sacrifice in this life. Nothing that we experience in this life—no trial, no grief, no suffering—will compare to the eternal glory we will experience in resurrection life. In 2 Corinthians 4:17 Paul writes that "our light and momentary troubles are achieving for us an eternal glory that far outweighs them all." Paul exhorts us to fix our eyes not on what is seen, which is temporary, but on what is unseen, which is eternal (2 Cor 4:18). This is a challenge to live out in the midst of suffering, difficulty, and uncertainty, but our future inheritance gives us the motivation to endure these difficult seasons.

The future hope of resurrection shapes our present experience. Scott Sauls writes, "If your hope is in Jesus, your long-term worst case scenario is resurrection and everlasting life. In the end, that's as bad as it can get."[5] Because our future is secure, this hope should motivate and comfort us in the present, and reorient our lives and priorities. In his first letter to the Corinthians, after his lengthy discussion of future resurrection, Paul writes, "Therefore, my dear brothers and sisters, stand firm. Let nothing move you. Always give yourselves fully to the work of the Lord, because you know that your labor in the Lord is not in vain" (1 Cor 15:58). Because of the hope and reality of resurrection, believers can rest assured that their future is secure and that their labor in the Lord is not in vain. And this is the reason that the gospel of Jesus Christ is good news indeed.

---

[5]This is an exact quote from Scott Sauls's Twitter (@scottsauls, May 15, 2017), but see his discussion of this reality in *Jesus Outside the Lines: A Way Forward for Those Who Are Tired of Taking Sides* (Carol Stream, IL: Tyndale House, 2015), 166-69.

RECOMMENDATIONS FOR FURTHER READING

BEGINNER

Allberry, Sam. *Lifted: Experiencing the Resurrection Life*. Phillipsburg, NJ: P&R, 2010.

Matthewson, Steven D. *Risen: 50 Reasons Why the Resurrection Changed Everything*. Grand Rapids, MI: Baker Books, 2013.

Warnock, Adrian. *Raised with Christ: How the Resurrection Changes Everything*. Wheaton, IL: Crossway, 2010.

INTERMEDIATE

Crowe, Brandon D. *The Hope of Israel: The Resurrection of Christ in the Acts of the Apostles*. Grand Rapids, MI: Baker Academic, 2020.

Gaffin, Richard B., Jr. *By Faith, Not by Sight: Paul and the Order of Salvation*. 2nd ed. Phillipsburg, NJ: P&R, 2013.

Keller, Timothy. *Hope in Times of Fear: The Resurrection and the Meaning of Easter*. New York: Viking, 2021.

Morales, L. Michael. *Exodus Old and New: A Biblical Theology of Redemption*. Essential Studies in Biblical Theology. Downers Grove, IL: IVP Academic, 2020.

Wright, N. T. *Surprised by Hope: Rethinking Heaven, the Resurrection, and the Mission of the Church*. New York: HarperOne, 2008.

ADVANCED

Beale, G. K. *A New Testament Biblical Theology: The Unfolding of the Old Testament in the New*. Grand Rapids, MI: Baker Academic, 2011.

Gaffin, Richard B., Jr. *Resurrection and Redemption: A Study in Paul's Soteriology*. Phillipsburg, NJ: P&R, 1987.

Vos, Geerhardus. *The Pauline Eschatology*. 1930. Reprint, Phillipsburg, NJ: P&R, 1994.

Wright, N. T. *The Resurrection of the Son of God*. Minneapolis: Fortress, 2003.

DISCUSSION QUESTIONS

INTRODUCTION

1. In your estimation, has the sacrificial death of Christ received more attention than the resurrection of Christ in teaching and theology? If so, why do you think this is the case?

2. Why is the resurrection of Jesus Christ important? Is the Christian faith dependent on the bodily resurrection of Jesus?

CHAPTER 1

1. Discuss God's purposes for humanity. How do these purposes demonstrate God's goodness and the wonderful privileges and gifts God bestowed on humanity?

2. How are God's other purposes for humanity connected with his life-giving purpose for humanity?

CHAPTER 2

1. Discuss the consequences of the fall in relation to God's purposes for humanity. Why are these consequences so devastating?

2. Why is the first preaching of the gospel in Genesis 3:15 important? What is the significance of this promise for God's plan of redemption?

CHAPTER 3

1. How do the books of the Pentateuch and the Old Testament historical books provide glimpses of God's plan to provide resurrection for his people?

2. Discuss how the exodus event (leaving Egypt and going into the land of promise) is a movement from death to life.

CHAPTER 4

1. Martin Luther referred to the book of Psalms as "a little Bible." Why did he say this?

2. What do you love about the psalms? How have the psalms provided encouragement and hope for you?

3. How does the book of Psalms promise and provide hope for life after death? Why was this important for the psalmists? Why is this hope important for us?

CHAPTER 5

1. How are the future hopes of the Old Testament prophetic books linked with God's original purposes for humanity?

2. Why do the prophets so often connect resurrection hopes with restoration promises? How do the salvation hopes in the Old Testament prophetic books represent even greater realities than the old-covenant experience?

CHAPTER 6

1. Discuss how Jesus (in his person and work) represents the fulfillment of humanity's redemptive hopes.

2. How does Jesus' sacrificial death fulfill Old Testament pictures and promises? How is Jesus' death on the cross essential for God's plan to bring life to his people?

CHAPTER 7

1. Why is the resurrection of Jesus necessary and essential for salvation?

2. How has your understanding of the importance of Jesus' resurrection changed?

3. How might the resurrection of Jesus shape and impact your life and ministry? How can we emphasize the importance of Jesus' resurrection in ministry and teaching?

CHAPTER 8

1. Discuss the significance of the present spiritual resurrection of believers. What does it mean for our present lives? What does it mean for our future hopes?

2. How is the spiritual resurrection of believers connected with the new life in the Spirit? How does this help you understand and apply, for example, Paul's exhortations to walk by the Spirit (Gal 5:16), to live by the Spirit (Gal 5:25; Rom 8:5, 13), to keep in step with the Spirit (Gal 5:25), and to sow to please the Spirit (Gal 6:8)?

CHAPTER 9

1. How do the second coming of Jesus and the new creation represent the ultimate hope for believers? How will God's purposes for humanity find their complete and final fulfillment in the new creation?

2. Why is the future and glorified resurrection of believers such an important and precious doctrine? How does this shape your understanding of eternal life in the new creation?

CHAPTER 10

1. Discuss Paul's teaching in Philippians 3:7-14. Why is resurrection a primary goal for Christians?

2. How should the doctrine of resurrection shape our lives, ministries, and perspectives in the present?

NAME INDEX

SCRIPTURE INDEX